The Fundamentals of Quitting Golf

The Fundamentals of Quitting Golf

David Divot

iUniverse, Inc.

New York Lincoln Shanghai

The Fundamentals of Quitting Golf

iUniverse, Inc.

For information address:
iUniverse, Inc.
2021 Pine Lake Road, Suite 100
Lincoln, NE 68512
www.iuniverse.com

ISBN: 0-595-32101-1

Printed in the United States of America

To Adrian, Jay, Erica, Gena,
Eric, Jean, Shirley and Irv,
who have all suffered from golf
in one way or another.

"He enjoys that perfect peace, that peace beyond all understanding, which comes at its maximum only to the man who has given up golf."

—*P.G. Wodehouse*

Contents

Preface xi

CHAPTER 1   Why Golf? 1

CHAPTER 2   Start Stopping 7

CHAPTER 3   Take Lessons 12

CHAPTER 4   Get Scientific 23

CHAPTER 5   Buy New Equipment 31

CHAPTER 6   Read Golf Books 39

CHAPTER 7   Alter Your Personality 46

CHAPTER 8   Subscribe to Golf Magazines 56

CHAPTER 9   Get Strategic 62

CHAPTER 10   Play Mystic 66

CHAPTER 11   Be Confident 70

CHAPTER 12   Have a Vision 73

CHAPTER 13   Join a Golf Community 77

CHAPTER 14   Go Mental 81

CHAPTER 15   Complete the Course of Treatment 86

Endnotes 89

Preface

○ ○

"The fundamental problem with golf is that every so often, no matter how lacking you may be in the essential virtues required of a steady player, the odds are that one day you will hit the ball straight, hard, and out of sight. This is the essential frustration of this excruciating sport. For when you've done it once, you make the fundamental error of asking yourself why you can't do this all the time. The answer to this question is simple: the first time was a fluke."

—*Colin Bowles*

Like most golfers, you probably want to stop golfing. But chances are, you haven't learned how to stop. "*Learn* how to stop?" you ask. "Isn't it obvious how to stop golfing? You just don't golf anymore. It's easy." But if you have already tried to stop, you know it isn't easy. Sure, you can tell everyone you stopped. You can put your clubs out with the trash. Or, as a more satisfying gesture, you can torture your clubs first and then put them out with the trash.

But most quitters end up un-quitting. That's because the subconscious mind of the ex-golfer has been listening to all the excuses accumulated during round after miserable round. Not only does it listen, your subconscious actually believes all the nonsense you have been spewing. So to quit, you must methodically prove to your subconscious that you were just trying to protect your super-sensitive ego and that all these excuses for your golfing were, in fact, just excuses.

This book offers numerous techniques for debunking the most commonly used golf excuses such as your old clubs, your infrequent playing and your lobotomy. But the following summary of the ever popular "I never had a lesson" excuse should illustrate this point.

Let's say your driver has just plowed a trench in the tee box and stopped a foot behind the ball. The members of your foursome say nothing and stare at their gloves. You make some joke about how you learned that trick shot from your golf instructor. Someone in the foursome takes the bait and asks if you have had lessons. That gives you the opening to admit, in pseudo-confessional tones, that you have never actually had a lesson. You go on to agree that you need lessons and that you know a golf instructor would change every aspect of your swing from waggle to profanity. You just can't find the time. Your execution of this excuse is flawless. This is not surprising since you have performed it on countless golf courses for many, many years.

Most importantly, this excuse has fooled your subconscious. Even though you have uttered it over and over, year after year, your subconscious has never questioned why you just haven't seen an instructor. Without a course of treatment like the one advocated here, your subconscious will continue to believe that you could be a golfer, maybe even a good golfer, if you just took lessons. This again proves that your subconscious is not playing with a full set of irons.

Like the keeper of an eternal flame, your subconscious will sustain this delusion until you have demonstrated again and again, and again, that the lack of lessons was just an excuse. You must prove that you could take weekly lessons for ten full years and still not become a good golfer. And, because your subconscious is your biggest fan, it won't accept a logical argument. In other words, you can't take five years of lessons and expect your subconscious to accept the abstract argument that five more years would not make your swing any better. You must take weekly lessons for the full ten-year course of treatment. You must hack, hook, slice and stub your way to freedom.

Remember that "I've never had lessons" is just one of the many excuses that you have been using throughout your golfing career. You must now unravel the damage caused by all of these excuses through a ten-year course of treatment. As described in the chapters of this book, you must study physics to understand that golf is not really a sport but a game of chance. You must search for secret golf tips to appreciate that if anyone really had a useful golf secret, they would definitely keep it a secret. You must learn that having confidence in your game is one of the surest ways of losing confidence. And you must find out that you could increase your time on the golf course until you live on the course, quite literally, and you would still not be able to golf.

There is no easy way out. But it's worth the effort. You *can* quit!

1

Why Golf?

"My best score was 103, but I've only been playing for 15 years."

—*Alex Karris*

Over 37 million Americans are currently afflicted by golf. That's more than one out of every eight U.S. citizens. In addition, one million new people contract golf every year.

Despite these statistics, the federal government has shown little interest in studying this epidemic. And the pharmaceutical industry has yet to even test golf-suppressing drugs in pill, gum, patch or any other form. Consequently, the course of treatment recommended in this book is one of few tools currently available to golf sufferers.

But before describing this treatment, we need to consider the reasons why people start golfing in the first place. When asked this question, many golfers report that they like the exercise or the challenge of the game. Some actually say that golf is fun. As your first step toward a golf-free life, read the following examinations of these responses. Then ask yourself whether you agree that there is no good excuse for golf.

"Golf Is Good for My Health"

Mark Twain once quipped that golf was a "good walk spoiled." Of course, Twain wrote that before the advent of the motorized golf cart. Using a golf cart, you forego the "good walk" that might actually provide some beneficial exercise. That leaves you with just the hacking, chopping and yipping, in other words, the "spoiled" stuff.

Even walking the course, golf's exercise benefits are inevitably offset by score-induced stress. Non-golfers assume that the bright-red faces on golfers indicate vigorous activity or possibly sunburn. But, unfortunately, the flushed skin and bulging veins really indicate how the golfer's hypertension is reacting to his slicing, stubbing and four-putting. For many golfers, the key objective of a round is not par but a blood pressure reading that that won't blow the mercury out of a sphygmomanometer. In fact, some doctors advise that, from a health standpoint, it would be safer to stay off the golf course and spend weekends in front of the television munching fatty, salty, snack foods.

Golf is not the most efficient way of getting exercise. Some estimate that the workout from walking 18 holes is roughly comparable to that of playing three innings of baseball, one point of basketball or thirteen seconds of soccer. But if you ride a cart, the four or five hours spent playing a round of golf burns roughly the same number of calories as going to the gym and changing into sweat pants. If you actually stayed at the gym as long as you stay on a golf course, you could qualify for the Olympics weight lifting team in a matter of months.

So golf is not really a form of exercise. Golf is basically a thinly disguised excuse for avoiding household chores. In addition, golf is clearly a danger to mental health. Unlike many other sports, golfers cannot release their frustrations by playing harder. They can't throw elbows, blitz the putter or play any form of full contact golf. To ease their pent-up frustrations, golfers can only visit the beer cooler as often as possible. After a six pack, golfers may temporarily calm down, thinking that they are beating the course record. However severe depression occurs as soon as these golfers sober up and remember that the object of the game is to finish the course with the *least* number of strokes.

"Golf Is Good for My Character"

Perhaps you have heard that golf is the best test of a person's character. In weighing the credibility of this theory, first remember that professional golfers are the most prominent advocates of this belief. These pros are desperate to portray their life's work as something more noble than hitting a ball repeatedly until it falls in a hole. Next, consider carefully what golf actually does to your integrity, self-discipline, humility and moral stature.

By being absurdly unfair, golf invites every form of deception. No other sport would allow trees, puddles and sandy depressions to remain in the middle of the playing surface. But, in golf, you soon find out that these hazards are not accidental. They are placed there intentionally by famous, highly-paid golf course architects.

Furthermore, the rich tradition of the game dictates that the playing surface consist of living turf. These delicate blades of grass are expected to survive club-wielding hackers, lead-footed golf cart drivers and 250-pound golfers who perform their victory twist on every green. Considering the abuse they must withstand, golf courses should more appropriately be constructed of artificial turf or perhaps steel. But instead, we pretend that the all-natural playing surface is perfectly fine as we try to excavate our balls from foot-deep divot holes and watch our putts weave and bounce on a green that has more lumps and creases than an unmade bed.

Finally, wayward shots inevitably separate you from the other members of your foursome. This makes it impossible for them to tell whether your good lie occurred with or without your assistance. It also makes you wonder if they are improving their lies while you are considering improving your lie. So while enraging you with bad bounces, sadistic hazards and other evidence of inherent unfairness, golf simultaneously offers numerous risk-free opportunities to use your Foot Joy wedge.

Most golfers fail the integrity test, often several times in a single round and sometimes more than once on a single hole. They not only have ridiculously high scores. They also have to cheat to get those high scores. And to save their egos they not only lie to their golfing buddies, they lie to themselves. They begin to believe that the strokes recorded on their score cards bear some resemblance to the number of times that the ball actually moved during the round either by club, by foot or by hand. They feel perfectly justified in questioning someone else's recollection when they themselves have conveniently forgotten most of the strokes that occurred deep in the woods, deep in the trap or anywhere else that was hidden from view. So, as opposed to building character, golf actually creates a tolerance for relative truth.

To make matters worse, you can't practice the character trait of self-control on a golf course without inflicting further damage to the traits of honesty and integrity. Since most golf shots are disappointing to say the least, the average golfer is almost always angry or depressed. Yet golf expects us to hide our true emotions. Despite our anger, we must not throw our clubs in the water hazard. And despite severe depression, we must not throw ourselves in the water hazard.

Instead, when angry or despondent, we are supposed to simulate a smile and utter some acceptable platitude. Typically the platitude is an attempt to shift the blame for the shot to someone or something other than our lack of ability.

Excuses are a perfectly acceptable technique for cloaking true emotions. In fact, excuses are so common that some instructors have added them as the final component of the official four-part golf swing: back swing, downswing, follow-through and excuse. Consequently, in an attempt to practice the character trait of self-control, golfers generally resort to casting blame elsewhere, which hardly develops the character trait of integrity.

Of course, some golfers realize that excuses are thinly disguised attempts to shield their egos from reality, a cowardly reaction that should be used sparingly. These non-whining golfers deal with anger and depression through internal dialogs. Some golfers tell themselves that each poor shot, each rotten shank, each unmentionable slice and each inexplicable stub is really not proof of incompetence but a wonderful opportunity to learn more about the wonderful game of golf. In other words, these golfers lie to themselves. In an attempt to practice self-control, they resort to self-deception.

Some claim to golf not despite the humiliation it causes but *because* of the humiliation it causes. They explain that the adversity of golf shrinks their egos, making them better people. In the Dark Ages, human beings had only primitive weapons like hair shirts and self-flagellation to restrain pride. Perhaps no more was necessary, considering the average size of egos back then. Maybe these days we do need something more powerful to deal with all the self-importance that we have amassed over the centuries through our successes in science, medicine and television programming. But, as with so many things in modern times, we have gone overboard. Golf is more than just a prudent deterrent against the threat posed by arrogance. Golf is the equivalent of a nuclear arsenal trained on our egos. The humiliation potential stored in our ever-increasing stockpiles of golf courses has the capacity to vaporize every ego on earth many times over.

Maybe golf is necessary to deal with an ego the size of Donald Trump's. But in the unlikely event that mortification is your motivation for golfing, ask yourself the following questions. Doesn't your boss make you feel sufficiently insignificant? Isn't your ego adequately punished by your personal relationships, your work and everyday life in general? Are you really looking for your 15 minutes of fame or would you just be happy if the clerk at your dry cleaners remembered you from week to week?

Finally, what about the character trait of morality, or doing the right thing? Many scratch golfers remain scratch golfers by neglecting their jobs, abandoning their families and fleeing their real responsibilities for the fantasy of the fairways. In other words, their low golf scores reveal highly distorted priorities. From this standpoint, if the game were actually a test of character, the higher your golf score, the better. But, in fact, golf is really *not* a true test of character. It's just a test of how well you can hit a ball with a stick.

"Golf Is Fun"

The most commonly offered reason for playing golf is that it is fun. Anyone who has ever seen a golf course knows this is not true. Wherever you look, golfers are beating the ground with their clubs and cursing through clenched teeth. It resembles a painting of the tortures of hell by Hieronymus Bosch.

At least once during every round, someone will say they aren't out on the course to play well but rather to enjoy the fresh air, the companionship and the beautiful surroundings. These people mean well of course. But if that's true, why don't they just take a walk in a park with a friend? These people have been brainwashed. They can't see that golf is essentially torture. And torture, even in a pleasant, beautifully landscaped, park-like setting is still, basically, torture.

Admittedly, in every round of golf, even a high-handicap golfer hits a handful of decent shots. In other words average golfers are happy with the equivalent of one hole worth of shots even though these shots never actually occur sequentially, on the same hole. But that satisfying hole is only one out of eighteen. The other 95 percent of the time, average golfers are unhappy if not downright miserable. What other activity would we consider "fun" if we only enjoyed it five percent of the time? Would we claim that meals were fun if only one bite out of 18 was tasty, or even edible? Would we go to movies if we thought that 17 out of 18 scenes would be mostly unpleasant? If we forced convicted criminals to serve their sentences on a golf course, would they file lawsuits charging cruel and unusual punishment?

Bumper stickers proclaim that the worst day golfing is better than the best day working. But everyone knows this isn't true. You can be far more miserable on a golf course and, worst of all, no one pays you for it.

Allegedly, golf is recreation. Consequently, we voluntarily swing a golf club on our days off, completely without compensation. But physically, the golf swing is an awkward, repetitive motion that does not allow for deviation or creativity. If employers forced employees to swing golf clubs on the job, the workers would be indignant about having to perform a tedious, potentially dangerous task that ought to be executed by machines. Grievance procedures would begin. Foundations would fund research into the association of golf and repetitive stress injuries. Legislators would hold congressional hearings on inhumane working conditions.

It's an old joke, but what would a visitor from another planet think about the role-reversal of work and golf? Most likely the intergalactic tourist would look at golfers beating the dirt with clubs under a broiling sun and assume they were convicted criminals sentenced to hard labor. Conversely, they might conclude that only good earthlings are allowed to go to air-conditioned offices and play on their computers day after day.

No other sport requires the delayed gratification that's taken for granted in golf. Hackers are told to expect misery unless they pay their dues with countless trips to the driving range and untold rounds on the golf course. But, the mere fact that you are reading this book suggests that you have already been playing golf a long time, even though it may appear that you just started. Don't people start to like tennis in a few months? Isn't it true that many people have fun hiking with absolutely no formal instruction? Wouldn't it be more sensible to try a sport that you could actually enjoy after, say, five or ten years?

2

Start Stopping

o o o o o o o o o o o o o o o o o o o o o o o o o o o o o o o o o o
"They call it golf because all of the other four-letter words were taken."

—Raymond Floyd

So, you've decided to stop golfing. Congratulations. You have joined millions of golfers who say that they are going to stop, often in very colorful language.

But most of these golfers are actually unable to stop. Unable to stop? It sounds hard to believe. What could be easier? You just…don't golf anymore. You stop. Right?

Wrong. If you don't do it properly, you will never really stop golfing. You may burn your clubs on your outdoor grill one by one. You might find a new sport, or preferably several new sports, to fill the void left by golf. And, if all else fails, you could pay attention to all the things you neglected for the sake of golf. For example, you could shock everyone at work by actually attending a meeting when you say you are leaving the office to attend a meeting.

But just because you have rid yourself of tee times and paraphernalia does not mean that you have exorcised the golf demon itself. If you don't stop properly, sooner or later, the itch creeps back. When washing your hands, you absently practice your interlocking grip. You find yourself in your back yard with a rake, trying to drive leaves into a plastic bag. Then you catch yourself kneeling on your living room floor trying to read the break around a sofa leg.

You fight temptation, but thoughts of golf spring to mind every time you hear a four-letter word. You find yourself at a driving range with a set of rental clubs. By sheer luck, you hit three balls in a row without slicing. Your head tells you that it doesn't mean a thing. "Golf is just teasing you," your brain says. "Three straight drives, any hacker can do that once or twice. You just did it and you're a hacker. That proves it."

Your brain goes on and on, spewing the same old banalities rehearsed in thousands of hours on hundreds of rounds. But your subconscious isn't listening. Your subconscious is saying: "All I needed was a few months away from the game. Enough time to forget all my bad habits. I am back to that pure, natural swing that I had when I first started." And on and on your subconscious blathers, convincing itself that these three straight shots prove that you are an innately good golfer who temporarily went astray. Your subconscious then leaps to the conclusion that you are not only a good golfer, but a good person too and not bad looking either.

So once again, through the power of self-delusion, golf has got you hooked. It won't be like the last time you started playing again, you tell yourself. Or like the time before that. Or really like any of the ten or twenty times you unquit the game. This time, you will remain free of the destructive thoughts that made your drives and putts go roughly the same distance. This time you will let the true golfer within you play through the duffer that you used to be.

As you know, the irrational optimism that characterizes your return to the game is all part of golf's insidious plan to drive you crazy. It may take a hole or two. It make take a round or two. But sooner or later, you are playing your old game, slicing, sculling and even whiffing like you had never taken a break at all. And then your brain, which has been waiting for a chance to berate you, starts in all over again. Ridiculing you for thinking you could change. Mocking you for believing that you have any golfing ability. Needless to say, you find this internal dialog very distracting as you swing. You play some of the worst golf in your life. Before long, you are once again burning your clubs and declaring that you will never, ever again play golf.

The Paradox of Golf

As this snapshot of one stop/start cycle illustrates, when you stop golfing the wrong way, you find yourself on a roller coaster of high highs (based entirely on self-delusion) and low lows (based on the true nature of your abilities.)

Your ego cannot admit the painful truth that you cannot play golf. Of course, there is no rational reason why you *should* be able to play. The golf swing is a three-second ballet executed with power and precision, requiring a coordinated effort from every muscle in your body, including your brain.

Many pros admit that a golfer cannot consciously direct this ballet. Instead, it is said to be an instinct. But where is the scientific support for this "instinct" theory? Our predecessors threw rocks at mammoths, explaining why we have an instinct for throwing baseballs and footballs. And when the enraged mammoths turned on them, only our fastest ancestors survived, which is how our instinct for running evolved.

But where in our primordial past did human survival depend on the ability to propel a rock with a stick? Some prehistoric version of golf is unlikely as a hunting technique. What are the chances that our forefathers, without titanium clubs and high compression balls, were able to bean a saber-toothed tiger in one line drive? Today, we can't hit a green from 100 yards and it's not even charging at us!

If an activity remotely resembling golf was so central to our species, why have we not discovered a single cave drawing depicting a Neanderthal lining up a putt wearing a plaid loincloth or just breaking a stick over his knee?

Golf is not and never was essential to human life. Yet we watch the pros execute graceful, effortless swings and think we can do the same, despite years of evidence to the contrary. It drives us crazy. It shrivels our egos. We should run away from golf to preserve what's left of our self-esteem. But unfortunately, somewhere within our circuitry lies an irrational impulse to golf. It resembles our sex drive. However, unlike the libido, it does not ultimately serve to perpetuate the species. In fact, given that it leads some to think suicidal thoughts, the golf drive might even be the one human impulse devoted to self-destruction rather than self-preservation.

Clearly, more scientific research should be devoted to finding a cure for golf. With enough government and foundation funding, we might some day have a vaccine to finally eradicate golf so that it no longer poses a threat to future generations. But until that happens, we must fight golf using our current understanding of the disease.

We know, for example, that the subconscious mind is very impressionable. That's why all the experts tell us not to say anything negative on the golf course. If you call yourself a lousy golfer, your subconscious will take that quite literally and play poorly. Of course, if you call yourself a terrific golfer you will still play poorly. More research needs to be done on that as well.

But the point here is that the subconscious hears more than just honest self-criticism and disingenuous boasting on the golf course. It also hears every conceivable kind of excuse. "I'm using a new swing." "I'm using new gloves." My clubs are too short." "My back hurts." "My back doesn't hurt." "My caddie is too tall." "The barometric pressure is too high."

Excuses may seem like a harmless way of diffusing frustration and thereby averting damage to golf clubs. But the subconscious is listening to all this stuff and believing it. So when you try to quit, your subconscious continues to think that you could still play golf if you just had longer clubs or a shorter caddie.

When enough time has elapsed since you last humiliated yourself and declared that you were quitting, your subconscious will start to play these excuses back to you. Of course you won't even be consciously aware of these subliminal messages because your subconscious communicates subconsciously. For example, you might have a dream that you can't quite remember. It has something to do with you being naked at a party but then you realize that you are late for your final exam in chemistry and you never took chemistry. It makes no sense. But that weekend, for no apparent reason, you forget your solemn promise to quit and you find yourself back on a golf course. Despite all the club burning and the ritualistic burial of your golf bag, you inexplicably have just un-quit.

To counteract years and years of lame excuses, you must now prove to your subconscious that you can't golf no matter what you do and no matter how hard you try. As summarized in Chapter 1, your subconscious may incorrectly believe that you can't golf because you haven't taken lessons, or that you haven't taken enough lessons. So, remove that as a possible excuse. Attend weekly golf lessons for the entire ten-year course of treatment recommended here. Similarly, don't let your subconscious think that you could have golfed if you had better golf clubs. Buy the best set you can afford. Better yet, buy a set that you can't afford. In fact, spend an inordinate amount of time and money on the game. Prove to your subconscious once and for all that there is no excuse for the way you golf.

In short, to stop golfing you must play golf. You must also study golf, practice golf and place golf at the center of your universe. It's a paradox, an apparent contradiction that happens to be true. This paradox is completely consistent with the perverse nature of golf itself. Maddeningly, you play your best golf when you care about it the least. The slower you swing, the farther you go. The more beer you consume, the straighter your shots. So it should not come as a shock to you that to quit golf permanently, you must make golf your life for the next ten years.

Complete the Full Course of Treatment

Why ten years? Remember, again, that you are dealing with the subconscious. The subconscious is not a quick study. You can't just tell your subconscious to face the facts. It's thrives on ignoring the facts. Your subconscious still thinks you resemble your high school yearbook photograph. Your subconscious has built a whole fantasy world around one sarcastic remark from several years ago that it mistook for a compliment. It has no capacity for logic or abstract thought. The only way to make an impression on your subconscious is through relentless demonstration of your inability to play golf no matter how much you try to improve.

You will be tempted to throw away your clubs in less than ten years. However, that's like stopping your antibiotic pills when you are only part of the way through the prescription. The first few doses of the drug just kill the weakest germs.

If you stop golfing midway through the course of treatment, you just give your subconscious another excuse. Sure you took weekly lessons, spent every evening on the driving range and every weekend on the golf course. But after only five years, your subconscious muses, did you really give yourself enough time? It sounds absurd. But remember that you cannot be subtle with your subconscious. You must beat on it for ten full years or it will cling to the most implausible shreds of delusion.

You will occasionally have a good shot or two. It's inevitable. Your brain will panic knowing that the two good shots were totally random and fearing that your subconscious will blow it out of proportion, jeopardizing your recovery. Sure enough, your subconscious will be elated. It will feel vindicated for having faith in your dormant talent. It will assume that you have made a key discovery, that your whole game will now come together and that there is no longer any need to stop golfing. Your subconscious may even picture your name on the leader board at the Masters. When a relapse like this occurs, just continue treatment. In other words, keep golfing. Before you know it, you will once again be hacking and chopping and back on the road to recovery.

Stopping golf is hard work. Don't believe anyone who claims it is easy. Just don't give up. You *can* quit!

3

Take Lessons

o o o o o o o o o o o o o o o o o o o o o o o o o o o o o o o o o

"The reason the golf pro tells you to keep your head down is so you can't see him laughing."

—*Phyllis Diller*

Many golfers claim that they have never taken lessons. This excuse is very popular for obvious reasons. These untutored golfers want to give the impression that they might have latent golfing ability despite the fact that they need calculators to keep score. But they also imply that they are not competitive and therefore not interested in mundane concerns like winning, losing or even keeping their shots from hitting other golfers.

Most importantly, this excuse is commonly accepted on most golf courses. Your fellow golfers can't tell if you have actually taken lessons or not unless, of course, your instructor is out on the course with you coaching you through every slice and hook. And since it is never challenged, your subconscious totally believes this excuse even though it has been right there during the lessons you claim you never had.

To stop golfing permanently, you must rid yourself of the delusion that instruction would make any difference in your game. This book recommends weekly lessons for the entire ten-year course of treatment. Golf lessons are the best way of proving to yourself that golf cannot be taught, or learned for that matter.

Choose your golf instructor carefully. Good instructors realize that most golfers do not plan to join the tour but simply want to reduce humiliation when they play with friends and family. Avoid these rational instructors. They will make lessons tolerable, leading to momentary improvements during the lessons.

For maximum frustration, select a former drill sergeant, someone who acts like he will be forced to go on national television to explain why he was personally responsible for the fact that you carded a 135 at the Masters. This personality will ensure that lessons are as discouraging as an actual round of golf. And, of course, to maximize the pain, make sure the instructor is not only a golf nazi but extremely expensive.

Lesson One

At the start of your first lesson, your instructor will ask the standard question: "So, what is it about your game that you want to improve?" Perhaps, like me, you will say: "Just….everything."

Your instructor will laugh at your self-deprecating humor and ask you to take a few shots. If you're like me, after the third or fourth shot, his smile will turn serious and he will say something like: "I see what you mean."

Your instructor will be frozen for a few moments, wondering where to begin. Most of the time, he starts with something basic, like back swing, follow through or, that all-time favorite, grip. But, if you are like me, your instructor will decide that you have to crawl before you can walk.

So he says, "Just put the club down." He says it like a cop trying to disarm a gun-wielding fanatic. "Just put it down," he repeats, as if you might hurt someone with it. "Now stand like this." He assumes a pose with his back arched, butt out and arms hanging straight down, pointing at the tips of his shoes. You try to mimic him but fail. "No, knees slightly bent. *Slightly* bent. Your weight should be right under your shoelaces. Not on your toes, not on your heels. Right under your shoelaces. You briefly consider trying to lighten things up by asking whether he has a particular eyelet in mind. But something about his grimace makes you decide to say nothing.

"Are you sure my butt's not sticking out too far?" you ask. "No. That's where it should be. I'm not playing a joke on you. You don't hear anyone laughing do you? Get that butt out there and arch that back so that your arms can hang down and swing freely. Right. Just like that!" You feel briefly elated even though you have only learned how to stand.

"Now move your arms up and rotate your hips. Get your left shoulder under your chin and hold it there. Do you feel yourself moving in two different planes? Your hips and your torso are rotating horizontally. Your arms are moving up and down, vertically. Really, they move diagonally, but let's call it vertically. Now keep doing that so you feel those planes." What you are likely to feel is very stupid since you are basically raising your hands on your right and then raising them again on your left. You imagine that you look more like an inept cheerleader than a golfer. "Get that butt out," he reminds you. "No one's laughing at you. There. That's it. Perfect." You get that warm feeling again. Maybe you have a knack for this after all. Maybe all you needed was some instruction. Then you remember that you aren't even holding a club yet.

"OK. Let's look at your grip." Your instructor frowns. "You're letting your hands control the club with that grip." You silently wonder whether this is another trick. Of course your hands control the club. Without your hands the club would still be laying on the ground.

Your instructor twists your left hand clockwise and asks you if it feels awkward. You say "yes", thinking he will reposition it. "Good," he says. Then he takes your right hand and twists it counter clockwise until it feels as awkward as your left hand. "Do you feel that?" your instructor asks. "Now your hands can't control the club." You have to agree. With your new grip, the club seems totally out of your control. In fact, you're not quite sure whether the club face is right side up or up side down with your new grip.

"OK. Take a practice swing," your instructor commands apprehensively. You try to swing, but you feel like you're trussed up in a straight jacket. Again, your instructor winces. "Slow it up. Pretend the club head is a bucket of water and the shaft is a rope. You can't move that bucket fast. You've got to use your whole body. Ease it off the ground. Then stop when your hands are way up here and your left shoulder is under your chin. Don't start your downswing. The bucket will start back down all by itself."

You get overly literal at this point. "Won't the bucket fall on my head?" you ask. "I mean, it's on a rope, right?"

"Look," your instructor says as calmly as possible. "Some people find these training images to be helpful. But I don't think this one is working for you. Let's forget about the bucket. Just try to slow your swing down. When you get to the very top, let the club keep moving back so that your wrists cock. But don't start the down stroke yourself. Let it start all by itself."

Your instructor uses that worried expression again while you attempt to get the bucket and the rope out of your mind. "Remember to let the club keep going when you get to the top," he urges. "That cocks your wrists." With your old grip, you used to have a sense of what your wrists were doing. But now you feel like you're wearing handcuffs. You're not quite sure whether your wrists are cocking or breaking.

"It will take you awhile to get used to that new grip," says your instructor, with a flare for the obvious. "Keep swinging. Get that butt out. No one's laughing at you."

You flail at the air using your new posture, your new grip and your new swing. After several minutes, you ask whether you can try it with a ball. "Oh, I wouldn't recommend that," says your instructor. "It's too early to try to hit a ball." You explain that you have a tee time in an hour and that, like most golfers, you intend to use a ball when you play the course.

"I think you should cancel that tee time," he says. "You're just setting yourself up for a very frustrating round." You joke that all your rounds are frustrating. But your instructor does not relent. "If I were you, I wouldn't set foot on a golf course until you've been through a five week series of lessons where you see me two to three times a week." Realizing that he sounds self-serving, your instructor adds: "But if you absolutely have to go on the course in the next five weeks, at least practice for three hours after each lesson before you play. Trust me on this. You will become very discouraged if you try to play a round of golf right after a lesson."

Of course, what you have not told your instructor is that you hope to become completely discouraged. You hope to become so demoralized that at after ten years, the mere sight of a golf club will make you hyperventilate.

And so you walk directly from your lesson to the first tee. You deliberately avoid golfing with friends in order to maximize the humiliation factor. Instead you have signed up as a single and the starter assigns you to a threesome of middle-aged men with very expensive golf clubs. You shake hands with these men and struggle to keep from telling them that you have just had a lesson that completely changed everything about your golf game except perhaps the way you bend over to put your tee in the ground.

You insist that the others drive first. Sure enough, they all have beautiful swings and easily clear the water hazard that lies right in front of the first tee. You tee up your ball and make a silent vow that you will not abandon everything you learned in your lesson at the first sign of disgrace.

You rerun the entire lesson in you mind. Back arched. Arms down. Butt out. Weight under your shoelaces. Knees slightly bent. Reposition the hands. No, they don't feel awkward enough. Twist them even more. There, now they feel like someone else's hands.

Start back slowly. Hands are going up vertically. Torso is rotating horizontally. Let the wrists lock. Let the downswing start itself. You realize that you have spent probably a minute getting to this point. And this is just your practice swing.

The downswing isn't starting itself. You must be doing something wrong. Last minute check: shoelaces, grip, arched back, bucket on a rope, knees bent, knees bent too much. Wait, get that butt out there.

And that's when you hear the stifled laughter from the rest of your foursome. Your instructor lied. People *are* laughing. And you realize that the lesson is working. You are already discouraged and humiliated and you haven't even dribbled your drive into the water hazard yet.

Lesson Two

As you start your second lesson, your instructor asks whether you disobeyed him and played an actual round of golf. You admit that you did and that it was, in fact, frustrating, just as he predicted. You don't mention, of course, that you were looking for frustration.

"Let's see that swing again," he begins. "With a ball?" you ask. "No ball!" he booms." Without argument, you execute what you consider to be a pretty good rendition of his instructions. Your arms move vertically. Your hips and torso rotate horizontally. You remember to let the club itself start the downswing. And you follow through like you're posing for the cover of *Golf Digest*.

You look at him, expecting praise. "Let's review some fundamentals," he begins. "Fundamentals, "you think. "What could be more fundamental than swinging your club at nothing. But then, you recall the fundamental fundamentals. "Put the club down," he calmly says. Then he patiently tells you again how to stand. Knees slightly bent. Arms straight down. Butt out. You consider telling him that your foursome laughed at your butt, despite what he promised. But you remain silent. "And, most important of all, keep your weight over your shoelaces." "Again, the shoelaces", you think to yourself. "You picked an instructor with a shoelace fetish"

"You may think that you kept your feet on the ground during that swing", he says defensively. "But you were toe dancing. You lifted your right heel on the downswing. When you do that, your weight shifts too far forward. Golf is a game of balance. When you lose your balance, you lose everything." That statement makes you wonder. You thought when you lost your balance, you just fell down. Maybe, he means "balance" in the larger sense. Perhaps he means the balance in your values and priorities. Maybe your instructor is trying to tell you that you are just toe dancing through life.

Your mind snaps back to the lesson when your instructor barks out "Shoe-laces." You make a mental note to look for golf shoes that buckle. Your instructor has you pantomime a golf swing for the rest of the hour. "OK, that's enough for today. Remember, no golf course." You then realize that you have regressed. During your first lesson, you at least got to hold a golf club.

You decide to obey your instructor by staying off the golf course and visiting the driving range. Once you are there, you realize that there is no need to buy a bucket of balls. You don't even have to take the clubs out of your trunk to review your last lesson. You stand on the rubber mat swinging an imaginary club, hoping that this public display of absurd behavior will be embarrassing enough to help you stop golfing. But, before long, you notice that other golfers have stopped to watch your imaginary shots. They frown when they think you have sliced or hooked your invisible ball. Some put down their clubs and try to imitate your strange ritual. Soon, several of them are standing in a line, twisting their torsos and raising their empty hands first above their right shoulders and then above their left shoulders, looking like a choir of strangely-attired gospel singers. You make a mental note to quit this game before you too are insane.

Lesson Three

When you come back for your third lesson, your instructor sounds his standard greeting: "Let's see that swing again." "With the club?" you ask. He looks at you as though you are playing a prank. He wants to say something sarcastic, like "Most golfers find that the ball goes further when you use a club."

But he realizes that he can't remember your last session. "Do you want me to swing with the club....in my hands?" you repeat. "Yes, with the club", he says warily. You pick up the club with a sigh of relief. You were actually afraid that he might take you even further back to the basics, perhaps by restraining your arms and having you spend the entire hour working on your hip rotation.

He videotapes one swing and motions you over to a video monitor. You think you look pretty good as you watch your swing at regular speed. Of course it's a little hard to tell if you were keeping your eye on the ball since you weren't allowed to use a ball.

Then your instructor hits replay, promising to pause the tape as needed. You hope that he will at least wait until you start your back swing before freeze farming. But, to your chagrin, he stops the tape at the point where you picked up the club. "Now, what's wrong with this picture?" he asks. At this point in the tape, you haven't really done anything yet, so you decide that he is joking. "My pants?"

Without cracking a smile, he points out the way you slouch with your shoulders hunched forward. "You look defeated," he explains. "You should approach the tee with confidence. Spine straight. Shoulders back. Eyes straight ahead. You have to look like you are in control. If you can't even look like you are in control, the course will eat you for breakfast." You nod in agreement. But secretly, you cringe at the thought of having to spend the rest of the lesson with your chest puffed out, working on your tee strut.

Thankfully, after five minutes of this, he moves the tape forward a few frames to the point where you are now standing in front of the imaginary ball. Here, he points out some of your problem areas: spine, head, knees, hands, forearms, elbows and, of course, butt.

After a few minutes, he moves the tape forward another inch to the start of your back swing. Your behavior in this segment disgusts him. Instead of rotating your torso, you rock back on your right foot. Your left arm bends. Your head moves. Your hands strangle the club. Your wrists break too much, or maybe not enough. You aren't sure because at this point he has lapsed into golf pro shorthand and has simply cried out in horror: "Wrists!"

Your instructor continues, stopping the tape every tenth of a second and pointing out your flaws for several minutes. As a result, he is unable to completely critique your entire three-second swing during your one-hour lesson.

"We'll finish this next week," he promises. "But I think you can see that there are many things we need to work on." You detect happiness in his voice for the first time and suspect that he is calculating the income from hundreds of hour-long sessions with you. "And remember", he adds. "No golf course." You ask what you should practice for the next week. He quickly adds, "No balls. No clubs. I don't want you to make your bad habits any worse." You nod your head obediently, wondering if it is really necessary to go to the driving range to practice good posture.

Lesson Four

At the fourth lesson, you continue reviewing the tape of your swing from the previous week. You suppress the temptation to question putting this much emphasis on one swing. You know perfectly well that your flaws change from one swing to the next. On this one videotaped swing, you tucked your right elbow too close to your body on the downswing. But, on the very next swing, you could just as easily have extended that same elbow too far from your body. In other words, your swing is consistently bad. But each swing is bad in its own unique way.

You reach the last freeze frame. There you are, holding your follow-through and pretending to watch your ball slice into the adjacent fairway. It has taken almost two hours to point out hundreds of flaws in one swing. It doesn't seem humanly possible to remember all the necessary corrections much less execute them within the three seconds that it takes to swing a club. Your instructor agrees. But eventually, he assures you, there will be no need for conscious control. Your body will know how to swing all by itself. You try to verbalize this paradox. "So, your brain is not fast enough to actually control the golf swing. But, somehow, your body learns it anyway. Is that right?" Your instructor nods paternally and adds: "But only through years and years of proper instruction."

Finally, your instructor concludes that you are ready to hit actual balls. But first he advises you to adopt a pre shot ritual that remains identical every time you step up to the ball. By maintaining consistency, he declares, your routine pre shot ritual will elicit your routine shot. Considering your handicap, you silently ponder why you would want to evoke even one of your routine shots.

As a pre shot routine, your instructor stands behind the ball and sights an imaginary line extending from the ball to the exact point on the fairway or green where he wants the ball to go. He then places his feet on a second imaginary line parallel to the first imaginary line. He waggles his club exactly three times, and then looks one more time at his target and pulls his swing trigger. His swing trigger involves a slight forward movement that sets the rhythm for his swing. He explains that he silently hums a song to himself to replicate this rhythm, swing after swing. He won't reveal this song. You conclude that it must something by Wagner, probably *The Ride of the Valkyries*.

Now it's your turn. You stand behind the ball and pretend to target a small spot 200 yards straight ahead. In reality, you will be overjoyed if your shot just clears the tee. You put your feet on the parallel target line and start waving your club over the top of the ball. You realize that it doesn't look like a ritual at all but more like you are trying to shoo a fly away.

So, you try something more deliberate, moving the club head first up to the ball, over it, down the other side and back again. But that looks something like a religious blessing. Perhaps, you say to yourself, that's what this waggle really is, a benediction, or maybe a prayer that the ball won't go astray. In your distraction, your club waggles the ball right off its tee. In the process of reaching for the ball, you nudge the tee slightly. The ball now refuses to stay on the tee until you pull it out of the ground and reinsert it. When you realize that you have been doing all this for well over a minute, you attempt to make a joke by saying: "Don't worry.

That won't be part of my usual pre-shot routine." Your instructor just smiles weakly. He's guessing your swing tune is *Send In the Clowns*.

Then you experiment with some swing triggers. You try your instructor's little forward press, but you think it looks like you are trying to tango with your driver. You consider clicking your heels three times and saying "There's no place like the fairway." But finally you improvise on the gun metaphor and decide to cock your head to trigger your shot, even if it does make you look a little like a bobble-head doll.

By the end of the lesson, you are producing fabulous waggles. You think that you may have found a facet of this game where you excel. Just like golfers who gain notoriety as strong hitters or accurate putters, you could be known as a great waggler.

Of course, after each wonderful waggle, you continue to produce a perfectly miserable shot. Your instructor tells you not to worry about whether or not the rest of your foursome will find the discrepancy between your pre shot and your shot curious or even hilarious. He instructs you to continue to waggle like a pro and look utterly astonished when your shots go bad. If you play the role of a bad golfer, he muses, you will always remain a bad golfer. If you play the role of a good golfer, you just might become a good golfer. As he talks, you imagine your-self trying to express astonishment for each of the hundred or so bad shots that you routinely produce in a single round. If your astonished expression is identi-cal, it will look phony and undermine the effect of your accomplished waggle. Clearly you will have to develop and rehearse a wide assortment of expressions running the gamut from anger and despair to bewilderment and resignation. In addition to golf instruction, you wonder whether you should also get acting les-sons.

Lesson Five

At your fifth lesson, your instructor begins concentrating on your swing plane. You are to mentally create four checkpoints in your swing. This ensures that your club is not doing whatever it feels like behind your back while you are busy star-ing at the ball.

The second checkpoint, for example, is at the top of your back swing. Here you are to check for the following critical body part settings. Your shoulders should be at a 90-degree angle to the target line. Your club shaft should be paral-lel to the target line. Your right forearm should create a 90-degree angle with the upper portion of your right arm. Your club face should be parallel with your shoulders. You wish that you had paid more attention in geometry class. As you hold this awkward position, you dread that his next command will be to calculate the surface area of your swing plane.

"No, your wrists are bowed", he grimaces. "Do you see that?" You begin to twist your head, trying to get a glimpse of your wrists as they wobble above your right shoulder. "That will produce a hook." You move your wrists the only way that they can possibly move without breaking. "No, now you'll get a slice," he cautions. "That club face has got to be parallel with your shoulders." Thanks in part to your painful, new grip, you can't tell whether your club face is parallel with your shoulders or in a parallel universe.

Your instructor suddenly praises you for mastering the swing and declares that you are now ready to tackle other aspects of the game. You wonder what he is up to since your swing still has all the grace and flow of a carved figurine in a cuckoo clock. Then you realize that he is afraid that you are on the verge of quitting your expensive lessons.

Unexpectedly, you are on the practice green, learning the mysteries of putting. To divert your mind from thoughts of quitting, he explains that putting is not about swing mechanics but about inexplicable qualities like touch and feel. You are so happy to be off the driving range that you don't ask him how he intends to explain the inexplicable.

Having promised not to discuss mechanics, your instructor tells you that the putting grip is exactly the opposite of the full-swing grip. The putting grip discourages wrist movement, which is notoriously inconsistent for short distances. Keep your wrists and arms rigid, he counsels, and rely on your shoulders. That's right, your shoulders. You ask yourself why you should entrust the most important shot in the entire game to a part of your body that you have never before relied on for anything, other than to keep your shirts from sliding down your chest.

To keep your hands working together, your instructor explains, place your palms so they face each other. Remembering the full-swing grip, you assume that this palm placement should be done in the most painful way possible, perhaps with the right palm on the left side of the shaft and the left palm on the right side of the shaft. But, remarkably, your instructor says that you can accomplish this in any way that feels most comfortable to you. You wonder if you heard him right. A comfortable grip is too logical for golf.

But having said that, your instructor threatens that if your wrists move, he will make you use the cross-handed grip. Picturing a grip of astonishing awkwardness, you swear that you will never, ever bend your wrists. You will use removable splints or wear wrist corsets. Anything but the cross-handed grip.

Your instructor tells you that the proper target line requires consideration of several variables including ball speed, slope, grass type, grain direction, prevailing winds, time of day, location of water bodies and, of course, defects in your putting stroke. You consider the absurdity of trying to estimate and adjust for all these factors and facetiously ask if that's all. He is completely serious when he tells you to master these variables first before worrying about the more subtle variables such as the gravitational forces associated with different phases of the moon.

And whatever you do, he cautions grimly, don't get the yips. Without waiting for you to ask, he explains that the yips are jerky movements that create inexplicable shots, much like your drives you think. And once you get the yips, he mutters, you always have them. He has a woebegone look in his eyes. You suddenly realize that your instructor is a yipper. That's why, despite his perfect swing, he is stuck giving lessons to the likes of you. And you also suspect something else. He too has tried unsuccessfully to quit golfing.

Ten More Years of Lessons

Somewhere after Lesson 100, it will be clear that you aren't improving. At this point, your instructor may begin to feel guilty about all the money you've spent without any noticeable benefit. He may suggest that you try another instructor. Whatever you do, don't switch. You don't want to lose an instructor who hasn't even thought of letting you swing in some way that wasn't extremely painful.

After another 100 or so lessons, your instructor may tactfully ask if you have ever considered quitting the game. This is a critical moment. Remember that you must complete the entire ten-year course of treatment in order to convince your subconscious that you really do stink. Tell him that you think he has made great strides with you. Tell him that just the day before, someone complimented your waggle. He will be touched by your loyalty and redouble his efforts to help you. This will create great anxiety during your lessons, causing you to regress back to the point where you spend entire sessions working on ball washing and tee insertion.

4

Get Scientific

○ ○
"You should always throw a club ahead of you so that you don't have to walk any extra distance to get it."

—Tommy Bolt

For centuries, humans have been baffled by the enigma of golf. Why are golf balls attracted to water? Why does it take the same number of strokes for a golf ball to travel the last five feet of a hole as the first 500 feet? Why do we keep playing this game?

Recently, the finest scientific minds have applied their formulas and experimental techniques to golf. These researchers set out to lengthen drives and improve putting accuracy. You must study this research and attempt to apply the findings. If you don't do this, your subconscious will stubbornly cling to the misconception that your lousy game stems from under-utilization of your left brain.

Don't worry that this scientific approach might actually improve your game and upset your plans to quit. The research findings prove that the golf swing is more complicated than the space-time continuum. One physicist discovered that most perfectly stroked putts fail to drop and that only one ball out of 24 can even travel in a straight line. This may make you wonder whether golf should really be considered as a sport or, more appropriately, as a game of chance. Consequently, science can be a very effective remedy in the treatment of golf.

Einstein on Golf

For example, look at *The Physics of Golf* by Theodore Jorgensen. I say that you should only look at this book because you are unlikely to be able to read it unless you, like the author, happen to be a physicist. *The Physics of Golf* attempts to describe golf with terms like centrifugal torque, vectors, angular momentum and rotational acceleration. The discussion conclusively proves that golf defies explanation in scientific terms as well as plain English.

At one point, Jorgensen describes the scientific principles of the golf swing using a formula that covers two pages and features numerous Greek letters and several symbols that you may vaguely recall from trigonometry. Apparently a physicist golfer can look at this equation and say something like "Ahhh. Of course. No wonder my swing does that!" You, on the other hand, will look at this and say "Accck. No wonder I can't play this game. The formula for a tee shot looks more complicated than the launch instructions for a lunar probe."

Compare this equation with Einstein's special theory of relativity: $E=mc2$. You don't need to be a rocket scientist to figure out that the golf swing is more complex than nuclear fission and the time-space continuum. This could explain why Einstein reportedly never broke 100.

Rocket Science

Now, move on to a golf book that is scientific but written in English: *Putt Like The Pros: Dave Pelz's Scientific Way to Improving Your Stroke, Reading Greens, and Lowering Your Score.* Like Jorgensen, author Dave Pelz is an actual scientist. After getting a degree in physics, he became a physicist at the Goddard Space Flight Center doing research on the upper atmosphere. But after many years as an astrophysicist, he left NASA to unravel the mystery of why golf balls orbit the cup without falling in. Perhaps Pelz was seeking something more purposeful than the exploration of distant galaxies. Or maybe the exploration of the universe just seemed too easy when compared with the infinite conundrum of golf.

Pelz starts his book by stating that putting is a science and not a black art. But then he proceeds to prove, scientifically, that putting *is*, in fact, a black art.

Pelz invented a golf ball slide that he calls the True Roller. Golf balls are released at the top of the slide and roll out the bottom onto a green, simulating a putt. The True Roller will endlessly mimic the same putting stroke as long as the balls are released from the same point on the slide. And as long as the balls are perfectly balanced.

"Perfectly balanced balls," you ask? In the first of many breakthroughs, Pelz discovered that only one ball in two dozen is perfectly balanced. Furthermore, Pelz found that a perfectly stroked out-of-balance ball can wobble 2.5 inches off course in only ten feet.

Upon reading this, you may suddenly realize that you have been taking ridiculously inadequate precautions when putting. Sure you clean your ball when it begins to look like it's made of mud. And maybe you swap your range ball for a store-bought ball once you reach the green. But, according to Pelz, your expensive, brand-new balls right out of the sleeve could be as lopsided as loaded dice.

Do manufacturers intentionally make lopsided balls? Don't the same companies that make the wobbly balls also make putters designed to help you straighten out wobbly putts? Doesn't this violate several antitrust laws or perhaps suggest the need for a congressional investigation?

But Pelz insists that the ball manufacturers are doing the best they can to build round balls. It is up to golfers, says Pelz, to separate the good balls from the bad, off-center balls. To do that, he advises that you float each ball in a hot Epsom salt bath and poke it so that it rolls around and comes to rest several times. Each time the ball stops rolling, mark the top of the ball. If a different spot ends up on top each time the ball comes to rest in its little hot tub, you have a perfectly balanced ball. However, if the same spot always ends up on top, the ball is out of balance. With any luck, you will have such a great time bathing your golf balls that you no longer feel the need to venture on a golf course.

According to Pelz, 23 out of 24 balls are out of balance. Consequently, discarding lopsided balls is a prohibitively expensive solution. Some golfers scrub off the telltale dots and give the lopsided balls away as gifts, typically to their golfing opponents. Alternatively, other golfers read greens so poorly that they intentionally use the wobbly balls as a way of improving their odds of dropping putts. These golfers play with the 23 bad balls and use the one good ball as their water ball.

Perfect Putts

But let's return to the True Roller. When you reach this point in Pelz's book, you may wonder why you have never seen a single True Roller in use on a golf course. This is surprising since their accuracy could clearly take much of the guesswork and frustration out of putting. But, as you probably guessed, the USGA, slave to tradition, refuses to accept this obvious improvement in golfing technology. Despite knowing that golf balls are notoriously inaccurate, USGA prohibits this device as well as other aides that could greatly improve accuracy including telescoping rails and remote-controlled balls.

As it turns out, Pelz did not intend to sell True Rollers to desperate golfers. Rather, he wanted to prove, scientifically, that even perfect putts rarely go in the hole. That's because real greens on real courses are pocked with shoe imprints, ball marks, spike scuffs, bald spots and plain old debris. To the human eye, these small imperfections are hardly noticeable. But, as Pelz depicts, a 1/8th-inch heel impression represents almost ten percent of the height of a golf ball. So, imagined at a larger scale, putting on a real green is like trying to bowl on a cobblestone street.

Pelz has taken slow-motion movies that show how a putted ball hops and weaves as it careens from one obstruction to the next. The amount of hopping and weaving will vary depending on many factors. For example, the luck factor changes radically from one course to another. Pelz's True Roller sank 84 percent of its putts early in the morning at an exclusive private country club. But only 48 percent of the True Roller's perfect putts dropped at a private country club with "relatively low membership fees." Pelz does not report any tests performed on a public course. Perhaps the greens were so lumpy on the public links that he could not get the True Roller to remain upright.

To make matters worse, Pelz found that the accuracy of putting declines dramatically as the day progresses. In the early morning, before the start of a PGA tournament, 73 percent of the True Roller's perfect putts dropped. Several hours and 250 golfers later, only 30 percent of the True Roller's perfect putts went in the cup. This decrease occurs because each foursome leaves about 500 footprints on a green. By noon, you might have 25,000 footprints on the green, primarily within a 6-foot radius of the hole. However, there are almost no footprints within a one-foot radius of the hole. Pelz believes this "no-step" zone results from golfing etiquette. My own theory is that no one steps within one-foot of the cup because golfers are eager to grant each other gimmes under the dubious assumption that no one could possibly miss a one-foot putt.

By late afternoon, the cup sits atop a small hill surrounded by a moat created by hundreds of overweight golfers squatting, crouching, stomping and performing their favorite victory dances. So your four-foot putt starts in someone's poorly repaired ball mark, weaves its way through hundreds of shoe imprints and still has to be headed exactly for the center of the cup as it starts to climb "gimme hill" surrounding the hole. If it isn't exactly on target, the ball will angle off the side of this hill and roll back into the misshapen moat. In other words, even though they look very dignified and serious to the untrained eye, every green is really quite similar to the clown face hole at the miniature golf course.

At this point, you might expect that the rest of Pelz's book would be devoted to proposals for making scientific improvements to golf courses. Perhaps the characteristics of each green could be programmed into a computer which would analyze each putt and indicate where the ball would have gone were it not for ball marks, heel imprints, trampled moats and fun-house ramps around the cup. Yes, the computerization of greens would be a daunting challenge. But if we can put a man on the moon, surely we can design a golf course where a perfect putt has a better than 50 percent chance of going in the hole. And who would be better prepared to design such a course than a former NASA physicist?

However, as you read on, you discover that Pelz has no proposals for golf course improvements. And, since he makes a living as a golf instructor, his point is not that golfers should abandon a game that requires more luck than a slot machine. Instead, Pelz wants you to use his findings to feel better about missing putts. After all, as much as 70 percent of the time, it's not your fault.

At this point ask yourself this question. Do you want to keep playing a game in which you cannot succeed even when you play perfectly? Worse yet, do you want to continue golfing when you never know if the ball went in the hole because of a perfect putt or because a series of random obstructions corrected your perfectly rotten shot? Think carefully. Ponder the absurdity of trying to sink a 10-foot putt after herds or overweight golfers have danced and stomped on your line. This could be a pivotal point in your attempt to quit golfing.

However, if this thought doesn't work, keep reading Pelz's book. It contains numerous ways for you to spend every waking moment trying to sink putts under odds that are lower than winning the lottery.

The One True Putter Path

Putter path is the direction of the putter during the stroke. To keep putter path on the straight and narrow, Pelz invented a training device called the Putting Track. It consists of two metal arcs that can be adjusted to flank the ends of a putter through an entire putting stroke. When you execute a perfect stroke, the putter does not hit the metal arcs and you are rewarded with silence. But when your stroke wanders, the putter strikes the metal arcs, creating a noise that is intended to train the golfer and completely madden all those who live with the golfer.

Pelz does not discuss fanatics who may feel that a mere clanging noise is not sufficient penalty for straying from the one, true putting path. These golfers may attach electrical current to the metal rails so that an errant stroke delivers a mild shock. To promote even greater concentration, these obsessive golfers would only have to increase the current to the point where a slight deviation in putter path makes their hair stand on end or produces second-degree burns.

The second component of the putting stroke, face angle, is simply the angle formed by the putter face and the target line. The ideal is a 90-degree angle at impact. To ingrain this perfect angle in your stroke, Pelz recommends the use of the Teacher Alignment Computer or TAC. When you practice in front of the TAC, a series of lights tells you when your putter face is perfect and when it is crooked. A mere 15 minutes a day for six months with the TAC and you should be able to keep a pretty straight putter face.

The TAC, as designed, is only useful in practice. During regulation play, the fact that your putt went 10 feet wide of the cup would provide adequate feedback on your face angle alignment. However, USGA is right to be leery of allowing these seemingly harmless devices on golf courses. The next generation of putting computers might go beyond telling you that your face is crooked. With Computer-Assisted Putting, or CAP, your computer might automatically correct your face alignment as you stroke. It might also fix your putter path, contact point and velocity regardless of how ineptly you lunge and flail at the ball, resulting in perfectly executed putts with every stroke. Clearly the next step would be Computer-Assisted Drivers and Computer-Assisted Wedges all delivering flawless shots. Eventually, these computers would be installed on mobile robots. Golfers would ultimately begin to stay at home and simply send their golf-bots to the golf course to perform what would eventually be recognized as a menial chore more suited to a machine than a human. This, of course, would threaten the foundations of the game. Golf scores would become irrelevant. Professional tournaments would be meaningless. Golf instructors would become unnecessary. But, here's the bad part. The golf-bots, being smarter than human golfers, would eventually refuse to go to golf courses, realizing that the game was inherently meaningless and not worth their time. As a result, communities would find themselves with abandoned golf courses that have to be converted to schools, housing and parks. Only USGA's firm stand on the regulations can prevent this ominous future.

Fail-Safe Shutdown, or Yips

Perhaps you are interested in quitting golf because you suffer from the yips, or a tendency to jerk or stub the club when trying to make a short putt. According to Dave Pelz, "yips" is just a technical name for a neurological reaction more commonly known as "fail-safe shutdown". The clearest examples of fail-safe shutdown occur to people who survive a serious car accident. The survivor vividly remembers all the details leading up to the crash. But just before the moment of impact, the driver's brain turns off to protect the body from a level of stress that could cause a heart attack. Presumably, yip sufferers are consciously or unconsciously sure that they are going to miss all their short putts. They are also apparently so out of touch with reality that they equate the missing of a short putt with being involved in a serious auto accident. At any rate, the brains of these golfers believe that the stress of missing yet another putt could initiate a heart attack, or at least an embarrassing barrage of foul language. So the brain shuts down and, sure enough, the yipper yips.

It is not clear what the brain is thinking when it does this. After all, the yipper is conscious immediately after the yip. And the stress of seeing that your ball is still three feet from the cup is surely just as stressful as seeing your putter hit the turf several inches behind the ball. If the brain really cared about the heart, it would go unconscious for several hours or at least long enough for your partners to get you back to the clubhouse and pour a drink down your throat.

My own theory on this is that the brain only pretends to care about the heart. Perhaps the brain secretly envies the heart and knows that it can play little tricks on the heart because the heart is just a big, stupid muscle.

For now, golfers need to forget about the pathology of the yips and simply treat the symptoms. Pelz's prescription involves concentration and repetition of putting stroke fundamentals. He advocates no less than 20,000 good strokes with the ball intentionally deflected away from the target so that you think only about the stroke and nothing else. These 20,000 strokes can be accomplished at the rate of 100 per day, five days a week for 40 weeks, or roughly nine months. Pelz claims that this exercise works by training the body's long-term muscle memory. My own theory is that the Pelz treatment works by punishing the brain for playing little tricks while the yipper is trying to putt. After being forced to concentrate on waving a putter back and forth for 100 hours, the brain is likely to think twice before pulling any more yipping stunts.

The Science of Quitting

As demonstrated above, some of the best minds on earth are currently at work on the golf problem. These scientists are trying to improve our ability to golf. But they may end up unwittingly proving that golf is not actually possible. In this respect, golf could eventually be unmasked as one of history's great hoaxes, similar to attempts to transform lead into gold or to invent a perpetual motion machine. The big difference of course is that gold and motion, unlike golf, are actually useful.

We should all encourage and fund additional scientific research so that these discoveries are made in time to help the millions who are currently afflicted by golf.

5

Buy New Equipment

o o o o o o o o o o o o o o o o o o o o o o o o o o o o o o o o o o

"A professional will tell you the amount of flex you need in the shaft of your club. The more flex, the more strength you will need to break the thing over your knees."

—Stephen Baker

As you follow the recommendations of this chapter, you may question why you are investing thousands of dollars when you only want to stop golfing. Just remember the Paradox of Golf as it applies to equipment. If you fail to invest in any paraphernalia that promises to help your game, no matter how ridiculous, you give your subconscious mind an excuse for not being able to golf. You don't want some part of your reptilian brain saying "I could have turned pro if I had just bought that bubble-shafted, tungsten-enhanced, big-headed torque-meister." You must spend the money and feel the disappointment again and again to permanently prove to yourself that new equipment will not help.

Club Fitting

It was relatively simple to buy clubs a few decades ago. You could choose men's or ladies', right-handed or left-handed and new or used. Now, choosing from the wide range of golf clubs on the market is more complicated than ordering coffee at Starbucks.

In the olden days, a "custom-fit" golf club would be one that was not taller than the golfer. Today, golf stores call salesmen "fitters". The fitter will measure your body height, arm length, hand size, finger size and the distance between your wrist and the ground. After entering these statistics in a special formula, the fitter will conclude that you should have the shaft lengths of the clubs they happen to have in stock.

Serious stores will have fitters who examine the implications of your golf stance. For example, if you stand unusually close to the ball, the fitter may recommend a club with a steeper pitch between the club head and shaft. As an advantage, this special angle will reduce the tendency for the toe of your club head to hit the ground while the heel pivots to strike the ball, producing your trademark "HEADS UP!!!" shot.

Good fitters will study your swing path to determine whether you are swinging inside out, or outside in, producing lateral ball spin, better known as hooks and slices. It is possible to counter lateral spin by producing backspin. Clubs that produce greater loft will create this backspin. After watching you for awhile, the fitter may suggest that you buy woods with higher-loft faces to produce the backspin necessary to counteract your lateral spin. If the fitter says nothing about higher-loft clubs, you should not assume that you have a perfect swing path. More likely, your fitter does not want to reveal the amount of loft that would be needed to offset the side spin created by your "wheat-scythe" swing path. Your fitter may be worried about jeopardizing the sale of a full set of clubs once you realize that, to counter your side spin, you should be making all your shots with a sand wedge.

The fitter will switch the topic to club head size. Male golfers, desperate to get their drives past the ladies tee, are eager to believe that larger club heads mean more power. Exploiting this belief, manufacturers started an arms race of sorts, escalating the size of club heads every year until drivers started to look like parodies of themselves. Some experts believe that wind resistance will ultimately limit the super-sizing of club heads. But more likely, some clever designer is secretly working on a basket-sized club head with stabilizer fins, giving it an uncanny resemblance to the rear fender of a 1958 Cadillac.

After they buy them, golfers quickly find out that they cannot actually swing these cartoon clubs. Yet buyers keep these behemoths in their golf bags as a form of psychological warfare. On the first tee, a mega-driver owner will ask for the yardage of the hole while tentatively touching a head cover the size of a carryon suitcase atop a six-foot shaft. This is the first act of a mini-drama in which the prop club pays for itself without ever coming out of the bag. In the second act, another golfer reports that the hole is less than 500 yards long. In the final act, the owner of the club terrorizes the other members of the foursome by shaking his head and selecting another club, implying that the hole is just too short to use the big guy.

Manufacturers have realized that they can lure male golfers just by naming their clubs after big things. To give some hypothetical examples, a club that used to be called something like "The Gorilla" might now be called "King Kong". Next year it might be called "Godzilla". Similarly, the last year's "Cannon" might become this year's "Cruise Missile" and next year's "Thermonuclear Device".

This does not mean that clubs with power names don't make a difference. Imagine that you are on the first tee, swinging a driver called "The Straight Arrow." This name does not send you any subliminal messages about explosive power or superhuman strength. So, lacking any unrealistic expectations, you take a normal swing and send the ball an unspectacular but respectable 200 yards. In contrast, picture yourself holding a club named "Volcano." You can feel the raw force of nature itself in your hands. You rear back and swing so hard that you somehow rip the waistband of your expandable waistband pants. Naturally, you barely graze the ball with your supernatural swing and it doesn't even reach the end of the tee. Yes, clearly, the clubs with the power names do produce different results.

Club Head Composition

In addition to size, the composition of the club head is a major decision. Wooden woods don't have the high-tech aura of metal woods. But they can be potent psychological weapons during a competitive round. While waiting to be called to the first tee, your opponents may initially dismiss you by imagining that you got your wooden woods at a garage sale. They may even assume that you are still using the same set of clubs that you bought when you first started playing. But by the time you approach the first tee, your opponents may be wondering if you inherited your woods from your father or maybe your grandfather who possibly was some famous golfer or perhaps the inventor of golf. Your refusal to switch from these wooden woods implies that you are happy with your game. That means you must be pretty good. By the time you step up to the first tee, your wooden woods have driven your opponents into a mild panic. But unfortunately, you still have to play the match. As you hook your first drive less than 50 yards to the left, your opponents heave a sigh of relief and return to their initial theory, that you got your wooden woods at a garage sale.

Metal woods evolved as the scientific breakthroughs of the Cold War were applied to more important uses, such as golf clubs. Today you can choose between a wide range of materials including steel, regular titanium, beta titanium and "forged titanium with a cryogenic Superbeta face." At least one manufacturer offers a titanium face with a tungsten insert. Not to be outdone, a manufacturer named Diamond Touch offers a titanium head with a 20-carat diamond insert. Future models may feature your choice of ruby or emerald "accent inserts".

Club face materials are becoming so effective that golf associations have developed maximum limits for the percentage of energy that can be transferred from the club to the ball. Conceivably, any bans on illegal club face substances will be enforced through surprise metallurgy tests that screen for potential performance-enhancing alloys.

The golf associations apparently are afraid that unregulated drivers will make today's golf courses "too easy". Perhaps the golf associations should get out on a golf course sometime. The tour pros might be able to use contraband clubs to drive the green on a par five. But, for high handicap golfers, banned clubs could ironically make courses tougher instead of easier. That's because high-energy club faces simply allow average golfers to slice and hook their balls further out of bounds.

Irons

In the olden days, golfers didn't fuss too much about irons. Sometimes golfers would stick with the same set of irons for decades even when they changed woods as often as they changed swings. Pro shops could only fight back lamely with their commonly ridiculed phase: "Would you like irons with those?"

But then market researchers studied irons very carefully and noticed that they all looked the same, regardless of the year or the brand. Under these circumstances, what reason would people possibly have for replacing one set of metal sticks with another set of metal sticks? No wonder many golfers only bought one set of irons in their entire lifetime. Why buy a new set of irons unless you threw the old set in a water hazard?

Thanks to this groundbreaking discovery, you now have all kinds of irons to choose from. Today, irons, like woods, come in a wide assortment of materials such as soft forged steel, semi-soft steel, cryogenic super steel, stainless steel and titanium. One bi-polar set of irons even offers a semi-soft-steel head with tungsten inserts.

Now there are big-headed irons to match your big-headed woods. Many of today's irons have cavities. And since that term has negative connotations, particularly for golfers who grew up before fluoridated water, the backs of these irons explain that these are good cavities. You can buy irons with skinny soles and fat soles. Some irons boast of perimeter weighting, giving golfers hope that the entire club is one, big sweet spot, including the shaft.

Wedges

What could be simpler than a wedge? You are supposed to swing them slowly, so you should not have to worry about torque-suppressing shaft materials or high-energy coefficients. Yet a recent issue of *Golf Monthly* lists over 80 different models to choose from. All of these models imply an ability to create ball-stopping backspin even if your approach shot fails to get more than two feet in the air. A few club makers offer "safe" backspin-producing club faces like soft steel, Beryllium and even diamond coated faces, presumably for those very formal greens.

Observant golfers have discovered that rust on the face of a wedge also produces excellent backspin. Consequently, many manufacturers offer wedges that will rust over time or, better yet, come new with a fresh coat of rust. The warrantees for these wedges presumably promise you ample rust or your money back.

At first, it seems courageous for manufacturers to admit that rust is good. After all, why would golfers trade in their old rusty wedges for costly new rusty wedges? But these manufacturers know their customers. They know that old rusty wedges often misbehave and have to be sent to the garage for a "time out." And sometimes, rusty old wedges that are really bad have to be taught a lesson. As a result of these "lessons", many rusty old wedges sustain career-ending injuries and have to be replaced by rusty new wedges.

Putters

Golf club designers are probably as frustrated as car designers. There are only so many ways that you can distort the basic shape of a driver or an iron before they no longer work, or worse until golfers no longer buy them. But the putter is a major exception to that rule. A putter only needs to move the golf ball a relatively short distance. This is a simple task that could be accomplished by any number of objects, including the golfer's shoe.

But it is this need for simplicity that inspires golf club designers to use their greatest creativity. There are more than 200 kinds of putters. And, unlike, other golf clubs, putters don't all look alike. Originally, putters looked something like a bent butter knife. Then some daring designer went crazy, fattening the blade and curling the ends, producing a vaguely Middle-Eastern look. And that opened the floodgates of imagination.

Today's putters encourage golfers to exercise their brains by attempting straight strokes using bent shafts, often offset from the putter head to confuse the eye as well as the mind. The putter heads themselves sometimes resemble staplers, magnets and toy hammers. The manufacturers have not admitted the purpose of these whimsical designs. Perhaps they are intended to make the golfer subconsciously laugh, thereby reducing the tension that can cause sculled putts. Alternatively, perhaps these fanciful shapes are intended to help you laugh *after* your sculled putt. More likely they are designed to provide the golfer with a handy excuse for missing the putt as in: "It's no wonder I missed that putt. This new putter of mine looks like a banana split on a stick."

Balls

Until now, you may not have been too discriminating in the golf balls that you shoot. Of course, you hesitate to use a range ball, at least on the first tee. But everything else will work, particularly if you are on a tough course and losing them at the rate of one or two balls per hole. That includes the balls that look like they are still caked with mud after you washed them, the balls with your insurance agent's name on them and even the balls with gashes so deep they appear to be a cut-away exhibit of the ball's inner structure.

You may have heard that the USGA prohibits golf balls from exceeding a distance of 280 yards when hit by its "Iron Byron" driving robot. This statistic may not impress you until you realize that they mean 280 yards from just *one* hit. Apparently, if these limits were not in place, good golfers would be teeing off with their putters. As usual, USGA only thinks about the good golfers when it dreams up these rules. If it had the average golfer in mind, USGA would also require balls to go a *minimum* of 100 yards when hit by its "Tin Jim" robot.

As you probably know, surlyn-covered balls are better for higher-handicap golfers. Surlyn is a tough plastic that better withstands topping, shanking and ricocheting off stucco-clad, fairway-adjacent homes. But good golfers claim that Surlyn balls are too rock-like. These low handicappers prefer the soft, rubbery balata balls that they can feel. A high handicap golfer will not even understand how someone could "feel" anything when you hit it with a stick traveling at 100 miles an hour.

Nevertheless, you should buy the most expensive balata balls that you can find. If balata balls are truly responsive, they should respond to your unique "glancing blow" club path by veering, careening and performing loop-the-loops.

As a result, balata balls will help you ultimately stop golfing since the "feeling" they produce is likely to be that of embarrassment.

In addition, the balata material is relatively sensitive and can be damaged, some claim, just by sarcastic remarks. As a result, you will probably double the number of expensive balls that you need to buy, thereby increasing your pain and motivation to quit.

Tees

Remember to completely change every piece of golf equipment that you currently own, no matter how insignificant it may seem. For example, you may still be using 20th Century tees. These wooden pegs seem harmless. But research has shown that they might twist as you knock them out of the turf, imparting an unwanted spin to the ball. Of course, this tee-induced spin could benefit you by offsetting the spin that you give the ball in the process of your trademark "side-swipe" swing. Despite that, assume that tee-induced spin is bad and cure it with the "Willit", a tee that supports your ball on two pins. This design is intended to keep the tee from spinning madly as it leaves the ground. Golfers worried that even a two-pronged tee could gyrate might alternatively look for a steel ball support that bolts to a concrete slab ensuring absolutely no tee movement whatsoever, although a great likelihood of severe club damage.

Finally, some manufacturers claim to make tees that correct the spin caused by the golfer rather than the tee. With one model, the tee resembles a "modern" chair from the 1950s with a chair back that separates the ball from your driver. Your club face hits the chair back and both the tee and the ball are supposed to sail down the fairway. Since your club face never touches the ball, it theoretically cannot transmit pesky spins to your shot. To put it mildly, this tee calls for a clear choice between distance and direction. You have to ask yourself if it makes sense to buy a driver with a beta titanium face and then put a piece of plastic between the club and the ball. Why not eliminate spin entirely by just strapping a wet sponge to your club face? This tee will probably not become popular unless the USGA rules change, allowing you to switch after your drive and play the remainder of the hole with your tee if it happens to travel further than your ball.

The Complete Package

The Paradox of Golf requires that you buy as much new golf equipment as you can afford, and preferably more than you can afford. Each purchase will disappoint you until your subconscious is finally convinced that no amount of new paraphernalia will help. Of course, this step alone could drive you into bankruptcy. But that too will achieve your goal since you will no longer be able to afford green fees.

6

Read Golf Books

○ ○

"Golf tips are like aspirin. One may do you good, but if your swallow the whole bottle you will be lucky to survive."

—*Harvey Penick*

Despite weekly lessons, a new excuse may emerge in your attempt to blame everyone but yourself for the embarrassment known as your golf game. Specifically, you may question whether your golf instructor is using the right approach for your unique golfing style. After all, if your instructor is so great, why has he been reduced to giving lessons to someone like you? For special advice, you should seek the wisdom found in some of the 40,000 golf books currently available.

Fundamental Fundamentals

Start your tutorial with basic golf books, like *Winning Golf Made Easy* by Johnny M. Anderson. This book takes nothing for granted. In the second paragraph, Anderson explains that the goal of golf is to complete the course in the lowest possible number of shots. Pause at this point and imagine a naïve, young golfer who was very enthusiastic about his game until reading that sobering fact.

Next turn to a book that is golf instruction's equivalent of fast food: *Learn Golf In A Weekend* by Peter Ballingall. This book is refreshingly strait forward. In the Introduction, Ballingall claims that in one weekend you can not just learn the game but understand fundamentals that "will guarantee your enjoyment." After reading that statement, you will look to see whether this book is perhaps one in a series of wildly optimistic books with titles like *Play Professional Basketball Regardless Of Your Height* or *Lasting World Peace In Ten Simple Steps*.

Ballingall is serious about teaching you how to golf in one weekend, twelve hours to be exact. To help you meet that goal, he has assigned time allotments to each of ten skills. For example, it should take you two hours to learn how to swing but only one hour to master putting. Unfortunately, he stops the timeline after ten steps or he might have scheduled you to break par during the second weekend and win the Masters at the end of the third weekend.

Other authors are not as optimistic as Ballingall. It will take almost an entire week rather than just a weekend to learn how to play golf according to Harry Obitz and Dick Farley in *Six Days to Better Golf.* These authors urge you to find your true swing. You can feel the true swing by attaching a rock to a string and twirling it around. While doing this, you realize that the rock goes faster when you let your forearms gently create centrifugal forces. Once you feel the true swing, you don't have to tell your legs, torso, wrists or any other part of your anatomy anything. You just have to keep them from getting in the way of the true swing. This may give you a momentary feeling of euphoria until you consider that hitting a golf ball straight is a lot more complicated than swinging a rock on a string.

In *Mind Over Golf*, Dr. Richard Koop discusses waggles, practice swings, swing triggers and other gestures found in pre-shot routines. He cautions golfers not to mistake the pre-shot routine for the actual game. Nevertheless, some golfers get so wrapped up in these routines that they have pre-pre-shot routines to help them get ready for their pre-shot routines. Some golfers turn to teaching pros when they feel that they have lost their pre-shot routines. At the extreme, golfers who mess up their pre-shot routines have been known to stalk off the tee in disgust before they have actually swung at the ball.

Advanced Studies

Arnold Palmer has written a book called *Play Great Golf.* Palmer states that his method can trim as many as fifteen strokes off your handicap. After some fast math, you may realize that trimming fifteen strokes off your handicap will still leave your score well over 100 strokes. That's your first clue that Palmer's book is designed to help those who don't need much help.

Palmer urges you to stop and think before selecting a club. For example, you may routinely use a sand wedge whenever you land in a green side bunker. But Palmer advises that you inspect the texture of the sand first. Sand wedges have large flanges that dig into soft, fluffy sand without digging so deeply that you bury the club up to the grip. But you should use your pitching wedge, with its smaller flange, if the sand is hard or wet. This advice is particularly important at some public courses where the municipality can't afford to put sand in the sand traps or, even worse, actually paves the sand trap to reduce maintenance costs. If you try to use your sand wedge in these "asphalt traps", the large flange will probably bounce up and strike the center of the ball. These bellied balls will likely fly right over the green unless you are lucky enough to hit the pin or one of the other golfers in your foursome.

You may be drawn to the section of this book entitled Heavy Rough given your habit of "playing the whole course." In heavy rough, Palmer advises that you select an iron and close the blade to make it sharper for cutting though the grass. At this point, you realize that you have a very different concept of the term "heavy rough." To you, heavy rough is a place where grass cannot survive due to the permanent shade created by the forest canopy overhead. Your version of heavy rough requires a chain saw rather than a closed iron.

Palmer says that it is possible to play balls that are partly submerged in water. To prepare, Palmer advises you to remove your shoes and socks and put on your rain gear. Then he advocates closing the face on a sand wedge and knifing the blade downward with enough force to lift up a gallon or so of water along with your ball. If you follow this advice, you could save yourself a penalty stroke and maybe move the ball into shallower water. Of course, it may take you several minutes to remove the leeches from your feet and wipe the pond scum off your face. But being able to card a fifteen rather than a sixteen for this hole will make all the time, effort and cold medications seem worth it.

Shots over water are difficult under the best conditions. But sometimes, overhanging trees prevent a lofted trajectory and the proximity of the green precludes a punch shot. If you have nothing to lose, other than your ball, Palmer suggests a shot that he calls "walking on water". Basically, you hit a low iron horizontally so that it skips across the water. Since Palmer can literally walk on water, his ball will dance across the entire pond, pop up onto the green and stop a foot or two from the cup. On the other hand, if *you* try this shot, your ball will prove that it can't even swim much less walk on water.

Palmer's book includes instructions for making left-handed shots when you can't take a normal, right-handed swing because of a tree or some other obstruction, such as a high-rise condominium. To execute this shot, turn a wedge upside down, switch the position of your hands and keep your head still to avoid whiffing. Palmer advises you to practice this shot since it requires you to perform your swing in reverse. And since you will whiff this shot, you might also consider practicing your post-shot profanity in reverse as well.

Déjà Voodoo

From 60 Yards In, by Ray Floyd, clearly demonstrates the essential quality for winning golf: blind optimism. Floyd is a big believer in visualization, or "going to the movies." But naturally, it's easy for Floyd to "go to the movies". His movies usually have a happy ending. In contrast, your golf movies might be horror films with gruesome scenes of murdered putts and butchered holes.

Floyd also believes in the power of déjà vu. For example, let's say you have a lie that requires you to fly the ball under a tree, over some water, onto a green and into the hole. When in this position, Floyd simply remembers that he has been in this situation before. You have been here before too. But the difference is that Floyd's prior shot was successful. Consequently, he simply tells himself that he has already accomplished this shot and proceeds to execute it. You too have that déjà vu sensation. But of course you are recalling, in terror, how you took five strokes just to get the ball into the trap closest to the green. Then you launched your sand shot over the green and into oblivion. So, while it comforts Floyd, you are basically sickened by that sensation that you have been here before.

Floyd's optimism is obvious from his tips on putting. He says your goal should be to sink every putt, no matter how long or how tricky. He scoffs at the thought of just trying to get a long putt close to the hole. He undoubtedly would not approve of my goal for each putt: "Try to keep it on the green."

Floyd tries to calm your fears by saying that digging a ball out of tall grass in the rough is similar to hitting out of the sand. He thinks this is comforting because he apparently likes being in sand. In fact, Floyd was named Sand Player of the Year on three occasions by *Golf* magazine. And he probably received that award for his ability to get out of sand rather than get into it. What Floyd doesn't realize that you probably were only mildly concerned about shots out of tall grass until he compared them with sand shots.

The Golf Instinct

In *Golf My Way,* Jack Nicklaus repeatedly states that there are many ways to golf and that you don't necessarily have to golf "his way." But, with Nicklaus' victories in 18 major tournaments, it would be pretty illogical to ignore Jack's way and follow the advice of, say, your brother-in-law.

For example, Nicklaus says that good swings can vary in many ways. But at the moment of impact, the club face must be square to the ball. He describes his swing as follows.

> To me, the relatively easy way to play golf is with a swing in which the club-face starts square to the ball, gradually opens (turns clockwise) as it goes back, and gradually closes (turns counterclockwise) as it returns, until, at impact, it is again square to the ball. This opening and closing is neither excessive nor contrived, but simply the natural response to a one-piece take-away, a generous turn of the body, a free swing of the arms and a reflexive hinging or cocking of the wrists on the backswing, and a reciprocal set of actions on the forward swing.[1]

On reading this, you become very eager to learn how to square your club face with the ball after you have turned your body generously, swung your arms freely and cocked your wrists. Nicklaus explains that, if you grip the club properly, you will return the club face to the correct position *instinctively*. At first this sounds reassuring. You don't have to learn anything. Your body somehow knows how to do this. But on second thought, if you have never hit a golf ball squarely, you apparently lack this instinct. According to your dictionary, an instinct is a natural, intuitive, inborn tendency common to a given biological species. According to that definition your inability to instinctively return to the proper impact position must mean that you are not really human.

But another possibility occurs to you when Nicklaus describes his solution for hitting from uphill and downhill lies. Nicklaus advises that you simply stand perpendicular to the slope thereby giving yourself a flat lie. This sounds plausible until you actually try it and topple over. Humans, you reflect, cannot ignore the laws of gravity. Maybe Nicklaus is really from some superhuman species. That would explain why he can return to the perfect impact position instinctively as well as stand perpendicular to a slope without falling down.

While Nicklaus urges you to golf instinctively, Ben Hogan claims that you should golf *counter instinctively*. In *Power Golf*, Hogan writes: "Reverse every natural instinct you have and do just the opposite of what you are inclined to do and you will probably come very close to having a perfect golf swing."[2] Perhaps someone with Hogan's gifts will be able to do this. After all, Hogan switched from being a left-handed to a right-handed swinger and went on to win 62 USPGA titles including four US Opens and two US Masters. Anyone who can accomplish that should have no trouble executing the exact opposite of his inclinations during a two-second swing. Of course, Hogan's advice will not help you golf but it will help you quit. By trying to first feel and then reverse your natural inclinations, you will never really know whether your hacking results from bad instincts or good instincts that you improperly inverted.

Tiger Woods

Many books have been written about the great Tiger Woods. Some of these books dwell on the amount of work that made Tiger Tiger. This is of course depressing because most golfers really don't want to work hard. We read golf books to find those five-word tips that will magically and effortlessly change us into, say, the biggest money winner of all time.

In *Think Like Tiger*, John Andrisani recounts that Tiger was taught a drill in which you grasp either side of an empty range ball basket with your hands and swing it like a golf club. If you try this at a practice range, other golfers may wonder if your next drill will involve removing the rubber mat from the concrete pad and swinging that as well. But, apparently this exercise helps you feel the correct shifting of your weight and the optimum hinging of your wrists. You may come to like this routine so much that you go to the practice range, give the range balls away and just use your hour to swing the empty basket.

As a teenager, Tiger learned to visualize every aspect of his swing, including the instant when his imaginary club face contacted his imaginary ball. With that mental picture in mind, he would then set up to a real ball and hit it with his eyes closed. Needless to say, this drill violates golf's first commandment. His eyes were not on the ball. They weren't even open. Nevertheless, Andrisani claims that all golfers could benefit greatly from this drill, presuming they have good liability insurance.

Mixed Advice

Multiply your perplexity by reading contradictory advice, such as Harvey Penick's *Little Red Book*. Penick writes: "The best thing to do is to find a grip that fits you and feels good and then stay with it."[3] Did you read that correctly, you wonder. He advocates a grip that feels good? This is heresy. Everyone else recommends a grip that makes you feel like you have been handcuffed and shackled, not that you have any first-hand experience with being handcuffed and shackled.

In *The Best Golf Tips Ever*, Nick Wright collects the wisdom of dozens of golf legends. He suggests that you emulate Henry Cotton and practice your golf swing by lopping the heads off daisies. Presumably, once you have decapitated all the daisies, you can move on to the tulips, roses and all other plant material still standing on the course. Your swing skills will be further tested trying to fend off the greens keeper when he sees you practicing in the flower bed surrounding the clubhouse.

In *Master Strokes*, Nick Mastroni and Phil Franke describe a tip called "Thin to Win". They claim that you are better off when your club head makes contact with the ball a little too high on the ball, a "thin" shot, than a little too low, a "fat" shot. That's because a thin shot still has power and accuracy even though it will fly a little low. In contrast, a fat shot lacks power and accuracy because the club head strikes the ground before it hits the ball. Of course, high handicap golfers will want to consider whether this advice makes sense under the worst-case scenario. For example, you could easily "think thin" and end up topping the ball or, worse yet, whiffing, thereby disproving the cliché that you can never be "too thin". In contrast, when your shot is too fat, there is always a chance that your club will bounce off the ground and still manage to strike the ball. Even if a fat shot doesn't budge the ball at all, it nevertheless seems less humiliating than the whiff that could easily result from an ultra-thin swing. As pathetic as it may seem, when you "think fat" you know that you'll at least you hit something, even if it's only the ground.

Keep Reading

With over 40,000 golf books currently available, you will have to read more than one book a day to finish them all in ten years. In keeping with the Paradox of Golf, the more you read, the clearer it will be that no one can really tell someone else how to play golf. As an added benefit, reading just a fraction of these 40,000 books will leave you little extra time to actually golf.

7

Alter Your Personality

"Never break your putter and your driver in the same round or you're dead."

—Tommy Bolt

Lack of self-control is one of golf's classic excuses. Golfers who lose their tempers also lose their golf matches and, in some cases, their golf clubs. We don't know for sure whether bad golf is the cause or the effect of bad temper. But, either way, your subconscious has come to believe that you could turn pro if you could just get personality implants.

For this reason, you must conquer your fears, funks and frustrations during the ten-year course of treatment. You must become so brave that you look forward to your drive on the first tee with all its attendant laughter. You must hone your ability to remain calm on the golf course even if you have to grind your teeth to the gums. And you must learn to view failure as success. If you can do all that, and avoid being institutionalized, you will no longer be just a lousy golfer. You will be a lousy golfer with a scary personality.

The Golfer's Mind

At the start of his excellent book, *Golf's Mental Hazards,* Alan Shapiro asks you to take a self-administered test of your temperament. A sampling of the true-or-false questions will give you the flavor of this exam.

#39 When I'm playing poorly, a sinking, almost sick feeling comes over me.

#27 A bad round of golf can ruin my entire day.

#14 I often feel like throwing my club.[4]

There are no questions in this quiz dealing with elation or overwhelming satisfaction on the golf course. Clearly, Shapiro is not just a shrink but an actual golf sufferer in real life.

Your responses to these questions place you in one of six categories. Needless to say, none of these categories is labeled "Latent Pro Golfer". Instead, these six golf personalities can be grossly over simplified into Fearful, Angry, Manic/Depressive, Self Conscious, Control Freak and Lazy. Reflect for a moment on these characteristics. This list is not from a management manual on how to spot disgruntled employees who are about to "go postal". These are the various states of mind that we inflict on ourselves by voluntarily trying to play golf.

Theoretically, you can fall into several or all of these categories. For example, you could be fearful of getting angry over losing control on the golf course but be too lazy to do anything about it. But, for simplicity's sake, this chapter deals with each characteristic individually.

Fearful

As explained by Shapiro, fear is not as much of a problem as the fear of fear. So, to avoid panic, the fearful golfer must be able to control the symptoms of fear. For example, he notes that one symptom of fear is dryness of the mouth. Shapiro does not recommend the traditional method of addressing dryness of the mouth: a cooler stocked with frozen margaritas. Perhaps that's because Shapiro knows that alcohol may solve fear problems while exacerbating other personality flaws.

Shallow breathing is another important symptom of fear. Shapiro offers a step-by-step approach to taking deep, cleansing breaths. As you perform these breathing exercises, ponder that the flaws in your golf game are apparently much more fundamental than swing, grip and stance. You aren't even breathing right. It's a miracle you are still alive.

Once you know *how* to breathe, you must *remember* to breathe. Consider the irony of this. In the process of swinging a golf club, you are trying to remember takeaway, swing thoughts, zen mantras, follow through and dozens of other unnatural concepts. Now, you are supposed to also think about something that you previously did *unconsciously*.

At this point you question the attention given to breathing. What about other involuntary bodily functions that are just as important? Why not remind your heart to beat? Why not encourage your kidneys to keep filtering your blood? How about urging your gall bladder to continue collecting bile?

To remind yourself to breathe, Shapiro suggests a visual cue like the letter "B" on your glove, grips or golf bag. Consider what your glove would look like if you decided to use it for other reminders as well. Next to the "B" for breathe, you might have a "G" for grip, an "S" for stance, an "H" for head down, an "F" for follow through and a "T" for throw club. Or how about an "M" on your golf glove to remind you to pick up quart of milk on your way home.

Anger

Anger is a significant handicap on the golf course. It clouds mental clarity, making it more difficult for the golfer to convincingly cheat.

Shapiro explains that golfers are particularly susceptible to anger because, unlike many other sports, golf does not allow for the release of tension. If you are losing your tennis match, you can run faster. If you are having a bad day on the racquetball court, you can occasionally aim for your opponent's back. But, in golf, it does you no good to race to your ball; you still have to wait your turn. And, regardless of whether you think your golf opponent improved his lie, you can't start throwing elbows. This inability to relieve tension causes frustration, which leads to anger. An obvious solution might be full contact golf. But instead, Shapiro advises anger management.

Shapiro believes that anger on the golf course is caused by an overall lack of self-esteem. "Because you question your basic self-worth in many areas of your life, you have created in golf an opportunity to believe that you do in fact measure up."[5] This may be true, but it seems counterintuitive. Nothing could be more destructive to self-esteem than golf. It is more difficult to achieve a low handicap than it is to become an astronaut or a tenured professor at a leading university. After all, people are willing to believe the old chestnut that any American can become the President of the United States. But no sane person has ever claimed that anyone can grow up to win the Masters. So, unless you happen to be Tiger Woods, you should only venture onto a golf course if you are so satisfied with the rest of your life that you are practically intolerable to be around.

Too much anger can obviously ruin your game, and possibly an expensive set of clubs as well. But, Shapiro insists, a little bit of anger can help. Being in a state called "cool mad," he explains, can summon up extra energy and focus it on playing well. If you have trouble getting a little angry, Shapiro suggests finding something to get a little angry about. But, in my opinion, any golfer who isn't at least a little angry while golfing is apparently not aware that the purpose of the game is to complete the course in the *least* amount of strokes.

So the trick is to set your anger thermostat so that you stay hot enough not to stall out but not so hot that you burst into flames. For example, you might set your thermostat so that you start practicing anger management after you bring your putter up to your knee but before you actually snap it in two. At that point, begin applying Shapiro's "Three Rs". *Recognize* that you are about to make an ass of yourself. *Reduce* your stress through breathing and muscle relaxation techniques. And *reenter* the game feeling calmer. But once you have completed your entire ten-year, golf-quitting treatment, try the "Three Other Rs". *Realize* that golf is an impossible torture that you will never master. *Remember* that you aren't going to live forever and that you should therefore do something you enjoy. And *retire* from the game for good.

Before leaving this topic, be aware that Dr. Richard Coop, in *Mind Over Golf*, distinguishes between anger that is inner-directed versus outer-directed. With inner-directed anger, the golfer realizes that he was the one who stubbed the putt and, quite appropriately, berates himself for his stupidity. With outer-directed anger, the golfer unloads on some perfectly innocent bystander or inanimate object.

In a normal activity, you would expect an expert to urge people to do the right thing and take responsibility for their own actions. But remember that you are in the paradoxical world of golf. In this alternate universe, inner-directed anger is recognized as more difficult to control than outer-directed anger. Therefore you are advised to find a socially acceptable outlet for your anger other than yourself.

Dr. Koop suggests that it is acceptable, for example, to abuse a caddie after botching a shot. Maybe that makes sense for tour pros who share a percentage of their winnings with their caddies. But it seems like a labor law violation to unload on some poor teenager who makes about two dollars an hour for dragging your bag around a five-mile course and watching you attempt to golf. Of course, the pretext for blaming your caddie can also be tricky. A common excuse is that your caddie gave you poor club advice. The other members of your foursome may wonder how using a six rather than a seven iron caused you to whiff. But, poor club advice is a socially acceptable reason for venting on your caddie apparently even when you were on the green and your caddie handed you your putter.

Of course, very few golfers use caddies anymore. And yelling at your golf cart would be too transparent, even for golf. But, luckily another popular scapegoat is found on every single golf course: the greens keeper. If you sail ten feet past the cup, the greens are too fast. If your putt stops ten feet short, the greens are too slow. If, in the course of three-putting a green, you go both long and short, it was, of course, your caddie's fault.

However, the perfect whipping boy is the course architect. Unlike your caddie or the greens keeper, the architect isn't even on the course to defend himself. And because he is this shadowy figure that no one has ever seen, the architect can easily be demonized as someone who intentionally locates bunkers and water hazards where they will penalize exceptional golf shots. In fact, you can use this fall guy regardless of whether or not any tree, trap or other obstruction actually impeded your shot. Feel free to blame the architect for your shanks, slices, duck hooks and even your yips. Be as outrageous as you like with your accusations. No one will challenge this selection since everyone in your foursome is also blaming the course architect.

Manic/Depressive

Shapiro claims that there is a manic-depressive type of golfer. I myself believe that the manic side of this personality type rarely appears on a golf course. I say this because a sane golfer must have some reason for the elation associated with the manic state of manic-depression. In my opinion, any golfer who gets deliriously happy over a single good shot during an 18-hole round is out of touch with reality. And getting two good shots in a single round never happens. So, the most jubilation that you are likely to see on a golf course is a muted smile, which is far from manic behavior.

Of course, golfers do experience the depression half of manic depressive behavior. Bad rounds can produce depressions that last for days or even weeks. For this personality disorder, Shapiro recommends first that you refrain from calling yourself a loser just because you always lose. In other words, lie to yourself.

When that doesn't work, many golfers attempt to "golf in the now". In this approach, you put all the past, terrible holes out of your mind. You approach each shot fresh, with no preconceptions, perhaps like someone suffering from amnesia. Then, as each shot goes bad, you are shocked anew to learn that you're a hacker. After each disastrous slice and horrifying stub, you simply forget it and rediscover with the next swing that you really stink. If you routinely use this technique, your ability to forget prior holes will expand, giving you the ability to forget entire days, years and perhaps even decades of your life. Eventually, you will be able to play an entire round of golf in total disorientation, struggling to understand why you are standing on a golf course with a club in your hands when you apparently can't golf.

Some golfers overcorrect their tendency to dwell on the past by dwelling on the future. Positive thoughts for the remainder of a round can help your game as long as these thoughts are realistic. However, golfers have little use for reality, which is why they golf in the first place.

For example, after a terrible front nine, you have a choice. You can accept the reality that your back nine score will never be good enough to yield a respectable 18-hole total. If you choose that option, you can loosen up and finish the round with only a mild case of disappointment. However, as a golfer, you cannot distinguish between confidence and delusion. So you concoct a fantasy scenario in which you play the back nine like you've never played before. You start out by telling yourself that you just need to par every hole. After you double- or triple-bogey the tenth and eleventh, you tell yourself that you just have to birdie the remaining holes. By the fourteenth hole, you know you are at a crossroads. If you stop the fantasy scenario now, you might still avoid severe depression and slink off the course with just a moderate case of dejection. But, that would be too realistic. So you plunge over the cliff and tell yourself that you can still save the day by getting a hole-in-one on each of the remaining five holes, regardless of the fact that only one of these holes is a par-three.

Finally, Shapiro suggests that you view each defeat as an opportunity. He means defeat as an opportunity for growth, not as an opportunity to berate yourself for weeks. But in golf, maybe defeat just means defeat. Putting a happy face on defeat assumes that we learn from our mistakes. However, any golfer knows that you might learn from your mistakes but that doesn't mean you can correct them. If all golfers learned from their mistakes automatically, there would be over 30 million of us on the pro tour.

Self Conscious

Self-conscious golfers are overly concerned with the opinion of others. Because they struggle with an inferiority complex, self-conscious golfers look for foursomes of people who play worse than they do. In some cases, feelings of inadequacy can turn to despair when self-conscious golfers are unable to find three golfers who are worse than they are.

Shapiro is from the school of thought that says you should not worry about what the other members of your foursome think about your game. As long as you don't shank a ball into their shins, they don't care about your game, says Shapiro. My own theory is that all golfers have low self-esteem, at least when it comes to golf. So, the other golfers in your foursome don't care how well you are playing, as long as you are playing worse than them.

While you are looking for three people who play worse than you, there are at least three people out there looking at you as someone who might just be worse than them. This theory explains why you suddenly get more invitations to play when your game goes into a slump.

Of course, if you have very low self-esteem, you are just happy to be invited regardless of the reason. And, if you have very, very low self-esteem, you may intentionally golf badly just to keep getting invitations to play.

Control Freak

Some golfers are too analytical. They attempt to control every component of their swings and sometimes freeze up because they are trying to remember too many details instead of just letting go. Shapiro urges these golfers to be more intuitive. He uses the example of a golfer who hits a bad tee shot, tees up another ball and swings at it without thinking. In Shapiro's telling of this story, the second shot is perfect because the golfer was not over-thinking the shot but, rather, just letting it happen. Recall that you have been in this situation often yourself. You have hit many, many lousy tee shots and have immediately swung instinctively at a second ball. But, if you are like me, at least half the time, the second shot is as bad as the first. In fact, sometimes, even the third and fourth shots aren't much better. If so, you have proven that your right brain doesn't play golf any better than your left brain.

Lazy

Shapiro says that golfers who don't practice are unwilling to delay gratification. By "gratification", he apparently means a satisfying round of golf. But, as we all know, the average golfer is never satisfied by a round of golf. In fact, average golfers should logically be more inclined to "delay disappointment" by staying at the driving range and *never* going to the golf course.

While some lazy golfers have a fear of failure, others have a fear of success. For example, Shapiro mentions one person who didn't practice because he might then be good enough to join the pro tour and he didn't want the lifestyle disruptions that would ensue. I myself don't practice because I might then win the Masters and I don't look good in green.

But, in my opinion, if we have to work at golf, we may begin to confuse golf with work. We will get to the golf course later and leave earlier, regardless of whether or not we've completed the round. We may decide that some holes are unnecessary "busywork" and skip them entirely. Finally, we may start finding excuses not to play at all. We'll cancel our tee times, complaining of colds and flu. We'll have our calls screened to make sure the members of our foursome don't find out that we are actually at work when we should be out on the golf course.

The Zone

Shapiro believes that alteration of hazardous personality traits can help golfers achieve The Zone. As you recall, The Zone is that perfect state of grace in which you are relaxed yet totally alert, attuned to your surroundings yet focused on the task at hand. When you are in The Zone, you golf well above your normal game, effortlessly, almost magically.

Shapiro believes that even hackers can golf in The Zone at least once *as long as they put in their time on the golf course.* That qualifier reminds me of the old saying that if you left some monkeys in a room with typewriters, one of them, *given enough time,* would recreate Shakespeare's *Hamlet.*

In other words, the only chance a true hacker has of visiting The Zone is if he lives on the course and plays day and night. Even then, one lifetime might not be enough for true hackers. I would feel more positive about seeing The Zone if I believed in reincarnation.

Shapiro believes that playing good golf is related to living a good life. If we eat right and exercise, we will have the energy and stamina to play eighteen long holes. He also recommends a healthy mental attitude at home and at work if we want a good score on the golf course. If you are like me, you will find this advice particularly paradoxical. In contrast with your job, your family and all the other demands in your life, golf is not supposed to be an obligation. Yet, this activity that you voluntarily pursue, purportedly for enjoyment, routinely perplexes, frustrates and generally drives you crazy. So it is supremely ironic that Shapiro advises you to be well adjusted off the golf course just so that you can go completely nuts on the golf course.

Concentration

In *Mind Over Golf,* Dr. Richard Koop writes that another term for the zone is just old fashioned concentration. To learn how to concentrate, Dr. Koop offers an exercise in which you relax in your living room and look at a golf ball. Dr. Koop doesn't mean just glancing at it. He wants you to study the ball's seams, curves and dimples. When you realize that you are not really seeing the ball anymore, start over, focusing on the ball's logo, its size, color and texture. To test your ability to concentrate, look away from the ball to try to picture it in your mind. Then look back at your ball to see how well you did. Introduce a mild distraction by playing light instrumental music. With any luck, your wife will enter the room at this point, wondering why you put on the romantic music. She will see you staring intently at your golf ball and instantly leap to the wrong conclusion. Nothing you can say will convince her that you were only engaged in a concentration exercise and that you and your golf ball are just friends. This encounter, though stressful, could help you quit the game forever, particularly if your wife issues you an ultimatum to choose between her or the ball.

Dr. Koop claims that some golfers lose concentration when confronted with relatively easy shots because they weren't sufficiently challenged. Perhaps you doubt this since you feel overly challenged by any shot, with the possible exception of a gimme. But, let's say, for the sake of illustration, that you have an approach shot to an unguarded green from a good lie with no obstructions in sight. Of course, this never actually happens. But remember that this is a hypothetical example. According to Dr. Koop, you might not feel challenged by this shot and the resulting loss of focus could cause you to flub it. To counter this, intentionally make the shot more difficult. For example, pretend that there is a tree between you and the green and that you have to produce a fade to curve your ball to the pin. Even you will manage not to hit this imaginary tree. But in the process of avoiding it, you will send your ball deep into the woods. In doing this, you have given yourself a second approach shot that is not only challenging but impossible, providing you infinite opportunity to exercise your powers of concentration.

Noises often ruin concentration. The sound of a distant car alarm can be very distracting, for example, particularly if it sounds like your car alarm. Even the sound of someone jingling coins in his pocket can be unnerving. That's partly because of the noise itself and partly because you suspect that the jingler is jingling those coins on purpose. While you should be concentrating on your swing, you are actually debating with yourself about whether or not to tell the coin jingler to stop. If you confront the jingler, he will immediately apologize, say it wasn't intentional and then exchange a knowing glance with the other two members of your foursome. If that happens, you will take your shot thinking not about your swing or the now-silent coins but about the jingler's glance. Did that glance mean that the jingling was in fact intentional? Did it mean that the other two are part of a gamesmanship conspiracy? Does it mean that all three of them are out to make fun of you just because you are paranoid? After weighing your options, you decide to let the coins keep jingling even though they are starting to sound like the bells of Notre Dame. Either way, your shot is doomed. If you say nothing, at least you deny the coin jingler the satisfaction of knowing that he is slowly driving you crazy.

On the other hand, your failure to challenge those who thrive on gamesmanship may only embolden them. They want to see how far they can push the envelope. For example, if you ignore the coin jingling, they may try using the ball washer at the top of your back swing. They may rattle their clubs, pretending to look for a driver. They might put their carts in reverse causing that piercing beep right in the middle of your waggle. They might secretly dial you as you begin your take away, knowing that you have your cell phone on. And if you turn your cell phone off, they will make their own cell phones ring and conduct phony conversations while you have a mental melt down on the tee. To settle your nerves, do what most golfers do. Think of the prank that you will pull on the distracter when he steps up to the tee. Using this as your swing thought, your shot will be awful. But thinking of retaliation may be the greatest satisfaction that you get out of the entire round.

Goal Control

If you really could completely change your personality, you would be a fool to squander that gift on a golf course instead of becoming an obscenely rich motivational speaker. But of course, you actually will not change no matter how hard you try. You will continue to hyperventilate on every tee. Your clubs will still fly further than your ball. And you will still swear so much that you even embarrass other golfers. However, through your pathetic efforts to change your behavior, even your subconscious will eventually recognize that you are never going to change and finally let you quit for good.

8

Subscribe to Golf Magazines

○ ○

"In ancient times, when men cursed and beat the earth with sticks they called it witchcraft. Today they call it golf."

—Anonymous

In the 13th Century, the Dutch played a game called colf in which players hit a ball with a stick in an attempt to hit windmills, castles and other target buildings on a mile-long course. Today, many golfers still hit the homes, condominiums and other buildings that line our modern golf courses. Apparently they are not aware that this is no longer the object of the game.

Golf magazines are the best way of staying abreast of these kinds of changes in this rapidly-evolving sport. To find a permanent cure for your golf habit, subscribe to at least five monthly golf magazines. Do not just toss each issue on the pile after glancing at the centerfold. Read every article, study every ad and attempt each and every golf tip. By the end of your ten-year course of treatment, you will have tried over 30,000 golf tips. This should be enough to convince your subconscious that the only tip worth heeding is the one reportedly given by Sam Snead to a hopeless hacker: "Take three weeks off and then quit the game."

Training Aids

As you read golf magazines, do not skip over the ads and "articles" about swing gadgets and other training aids. Study these ads and admit that a part of you wants to believe their preposterous claims. This will help you realize your desperation.

For example, one training aid looks somewhat like a portable gallows. You put your wrists in a noose. The noose is supposed to teach your wrists what a good swing feels like. That seems plausible at first. But, linger over this ad a moment longer. Wrists are not known to be the smartest body parts. That's why most people only use their wrists as a convenient place to hang watches and jewelry. What if the wrists get the whole cause-and-effect thing mixed up? What if the wrists think that they are being hung in a noose and punished for staying cocked until just before impact? What if they think that you are trying to train them to snap at the top of your downswing or otherwise you will put them back in the noose again? If so, this gadget could actually make your swing *worse*, if you can imagine such a thing. Not to mention that your wrists could spend years in therapy trying to overcome the psychological trauma caused by this device.

Golf magazines also feature another training club that produces a loud click when you swing incorrectly. This club would not be needed during an actual round of golf, where your scorecard would be an adequate indicator of how well you are swinging. In fact, it is not clear that this club is needed on the driving range either. There, a bad swing would be evident when your ball fails to reach the end of the rubber mat. Perhaps this device is intended for use when you aren't on either a golf course or a driving range but just in your home or office practicing your swing without a ball. But, even in a home or office, there are better indicators of wild, erratic swings, such as broken coffee tables and lamps.

Another device places sensors within a golf grip to monitor how tightly you are holding the club. If you squeeze too hard, the grip chirps at you. Choking and wheezing noises seem like more appropriate sound effects. But perhaps the manufacturer was afraid that uninformed bystanders would try to perform the Heimlich Maneuver on the users of this gadget. In the future, this product might evolve to address multiple swing problems. In keeping with the non-threatening animal noise theme, next year's model might meow when you cup your wrists, bark when you pronate or bleat when you cast from the top. If this product does materialize, be sure to add it to your arsenal of golf-quitting gadgets. Since you will probably be triggering all of the grip's sensors, the sound track for your swing will sound like a promotional ad for Animal Planet. The cacophony will destroy what little concentration you have, ensuring poor shots and endless embarrassment.

You can also buy a large, heavy bag to hit with your club. You are not supposed to vent your frustrations on this bag using random blows. Rather you are supposed to place this bag, which is about the size of a footstool, where you would ordinarily place your ball. The bag stops your swing at the point of impact, allowing you to examine your alignment for optimum positioning of head, arms, legs, feet, hips, shoulders, wrists and brain. In reality, golfers only pretend to check their swing components with this training bag. They simply beat this bag mercilessly after every bad shot. Sometimes, they don't even bother to pretend that they are calibrating their swings. They just whack at the bag without even removing it from the back of the golf cart. Some golfers even carry a back-up bag in case they beat the high-tech stuffing out of the first bag while in the heat of "fine tuning their swing components".

Golf magazines advertise a hollow, plastic club that you partly fill with water. This club is designed to teach you what a good swing feels like. Or more accurately, this devise teaches you what a good swing would feel like if you golfed with a hollow plastic club filled with a quart or two of water. Unfortunately, once you learn the feel of a good swing using a water-filled club, you are right back where you started, trying to produce a good golf swing with a real golf club.

And there's a training device that looks a little like a life vest designed by the Marquis de Sade. Your arms are strapped into plastic cuffs at the end of aluminum sleeves that are hinged to something resembling body armor. This harness is intended to prevent bad, slice-and-hook-producing movements. In fact the ads brazenly claim that you cannot produce a bad swing while strapped in one of these. (What is not mentioned is whether or not the device allows you to produce any upper body movement at all.) USGA is unlikely to allow use of this device in a regulation round of golf. However, you could try telling your foursome that your psychiatrist has ordered you to wear this restraint to keep you from hurting yourself and others when your game starts to go bad. This explanation should work since no one would ever question the wisdom of putting a golfer in a straightjacket.

Golf Tips

When you pay close attention, the golf tip articles in these magazines will amaze you with their golf-centric viewpoint and their ability to belabor the most obvious thought. Every time you catch yourself believing that you have just read something useful, recognize how badly you need to quit this game.

For example, you may see an article about playing golf in the rain. Despite the fact that you have dealt with rain all your life, read this article to understand how little you really know. The author tells you that you may lose yardage due to rain-slicked grips. He advises you to dry them with a golf towel. Very good advice…obvious, but good. And what does the author say about days when it is raining so hard that your golf towel becomes completely saturated from wiping your club grips? Does he suggest that you consider quitting since the golf club could easily slip out of your hands, perhaps flying further than your ball? Does he advise you to leave the course before you succumb to hypothermia? Does he tell you to watch for the precursors of lightning, particularly if you are standing on a barren hilltop waving a three iron over your head? No, the author advises that you carry *two* golf towels so that you will always be able to keep your grips dry, even in a tornado. The author of this article is equally capable of writing articles with titles like "When A Rattlesnake Is In Your Line" or "How To Hit Off A Moving Lava Flow." In your quest to quit the game, pause after each article and remind yourself that these authors are golf's success stories.

Prize Money

Ponder the attention that golf magazines give to prize money and the income of professional golfers. Logically, average readers should be annoyed to hear that a 20-year old prodigy earned $5 million not by curing cancer or achieving world peace, but by playing round after round of golf.

Perhaps the magazines are exploiting the tendency of golfers to secretly harbor wildly exaggerated opinions of their golfing potential. Possibly, this preoccupation with prize money feeds the delusions of even the worst hackers. Instead of reacting with disgust, maybe the average reader dreams of quitting his job and making tons of money golfing. All he has to do is just shave a mere 30 or 40 strokes off his handicap.

Golf Course Glorification

Golf magazines work the adjective generator overtime when describing golf courses. The featured courses are always magnificent, astonishing, spectacular or breathtaking. And those are just the average links. The really special courses are awe-inspiring, exhilarating and even magical. These articles encourage you to pretend that you are engaged in a transcendent aesthetic experience rather than just hacking your way around 18 holes. As you read these descriptions, question whether torture in the most beautiful surroundings is still anything but torture.

But more charitably, the lingo used in these articles can come in handy when you need to sidetrack any discussion of your less-than-stellar score. For example, imagine that you have just completed 18 holes at the Astonishingly Beautiful But Brutally Tough Golf Course. You look for a way to get to your car without passing near the clubhouse. But your arch nemesis waves you in from the bar and immediately asks your score. Finally, reading golf magazines pays off in a big way.

"Isn't this course just magical!" you respond. Without losing a beat, he asks "How many pars?" You reply, "The architect here has really outdone himself. The way he positions the holes for maximum scenic effect. It is breathtaking." As you make your escape, you realize that it was worth it to pay the outrageous green fees. If you had played this badly at some course made out of a former cornfield, what could you say as a diversionary tactic when asked point-blank how you scored? Maybe: "I'm not sure what my score was. All the holes look the same here. I think I may have played the back nine twice."

Golf Vacations

Golf magazines are filled with advertisements for golf vacations. These advertisements never answer the question of why anyone would ruin a vacation by playing golf. Nevertheless, employers are typically delighted to hear that you are going on a golf vacation. They know that when you return from a golf vacation, you will truly appreciate work.

In golf magazines, the golf vacations seem to fall into one of three categories: the Compromise Package, the Theme Package and the Obsessive-Compulsive Package.

Compromise Packages are designed for couples. Or rather, they are designed so that one spouse can play golf while the other one does something less masochistic. A Compromise Package might be a trip to Hawaii, the Caribbean or even French Polynesia. The sensible, non-golfing spouse agrees to the package, thinking it might be fun to lie on a beach for 10 days. Some spouses may balk at this thought, remembering the times that they have overdone it and contracted sun poisoning on the first day. But, to counter this potential trip-stopping thought, the ads typically feature several alluring photos of fancy tropical drinks with flowers floating in them. This is often the clincher. If all else fails, the spouse reasons, at least I can drink for ten days.

The Theme Package is designed to appeal to golfers who want to rationalize a golf vacation by joining the inherently useless game of golf with something more respectable, educational or uplifting. One magazine recently described a vacation in Flanders, France where you can golf and view the site of some of the most horrific fighting in World War I, often simultaneously.

Before long, we could be reading about a golf course at Gettysburg where you can reenact Pickett's Charge with a good drive, a fairway wood and a nine iron. Or how about a course in Mexico's Yucatan Peninsula that passes through Mayan ruins where sacrificial altars have been converted to elevated tees. And think of the possibilities if a linear course could somehow follow the top of the Great Wall of China!

The Obsessive-Compulsive vacation packages guarantee that you will play too much golf in too little time. Some of these packages feature variety, such as 14 *different* courses in seven days. Apparently, this allows "vacationers" to drop the names of these golf courses at cocktail parties. Unfortunately, the course names are the only things they will be able to remember since the pace of the trip doesn't allow golfers to actually figure out where they are. "Oh yeah, I played St. Andrews," the golfer will casually mention at the water cooler. "That was the day we did the triple-header: Muirfield, Carnoustie and the Old Course. What was it like? It was, very….ah…Scottish. Yes, it's in Scotland…I think."

When to Cancel Your Subscriptions

The therapy of reading golf magazines is somewhat risky. On the one hand, you need to demonstrate to your subconscious that all the new practice aides, gadgets and swing tips will not improve your game. On the other hand, you must be careful not to get trapped in the fun house of golf magazines. If you find yourself sending away for the breakthrough discovery balls guaranteed to double your distance or your money back, its time to cancel your subscriptions.

9

Get Strategic

o o o o o o o o o o o o o o o o o o o o o o o o o o o o o o o
"You know what they say about big hitters…the woods are full of them."

—*Jimmy Demaret*

Consistent with the Paradox of Golf, you risk the greatest danger when you try to play safe. In fact, pretending that you have any idea where your ball will go can be one of the most effective strategies for quitting the game.

Golf and Chess

Golf is often compared with chess. That's not because chess pieces travel roughly the same distance as some of your drives. Rather, the pros are trying to express how in golf, like chess, you should always be thinking several moves ahead of your current shot and positioning your ball to carry out your strategy.

Many golf books would lead you to believe that there are only two basic strategies to golf: cautious and aggressive. Cautious golfers will safely chip their shots back onto the fairway rather than trying to hit through a grove of trees toward the green. In doing so, cautious golfers conclude that the reward of successfully negotiating the trees is not worth the risk of getting caught in the forest and carding a double-digit score.

Conversely, aggressive golfers never get out of trouble by moving laterally, at least not intentionally. Aggressive golfers believe that every stroke is sacred. If you don't aim every shot directly at the hole, you will be beaten by someone who does. This belief causes aggressive golfers to try their trademark "Hail Mary" shots, typically several times in succession.

Realistic Golf

These golf books don't mention a third strategy, which happens to be the one used by most high handicap golfers. In this strategy, golfers are not cautious or aggressive, but merely realistic. Realistic golfers always swing as hard as they can and aim straight for the pin. They do this not because they want to beat their opponents or set the course record. They go straight and hard for the pin because they have no confidence in their ability to successfully execute a cautious shot.

To illustrate, assume a ball lies 250 yards from the pin. The green is completely encircled by a moat. However, there is a flat, safe area in front of the moat completely free of sand traps and trees. Realists visualize each strategic option in their minds. They preview stubbing a cautious lay-up shot that forces them to cross the water with a low iron rather than a wedge. Then they envision the low iron inevitably sending the next shot into the water. Next they preview an attempt to smash a two wood over the water and watch it also dive in the water. Faced with these options, the realists inevitably pull out the two-wood. Their "strategy" is to hope for the best.

Realists might be rewarded for this choice as follows. They swing the two-wood as hard as possible. Sure enough, the club head doesn't make solid contact. But there is still enough brute force to create an ugly 150-yard worm-burner that comes to rest safely, 25 yards in front of the water. Now, realists proceed to make a mess of the rest of this hypothetical hole. But the point here is that their seemingly aggressive strategy produced exactly the results envisioned under the cautious strategy.

Strategic Golf

The realistic approach described above could be good for your ego and, therefore, bad for your attempts to stop golfing. Instead, faithfully follow the advice of the strategy gurus. Plan each hole as though you have some control over where the ball will go.

Starting on the tee, the strategy gurus remind you that you don't have to tee up exactly between the ball markers. You probably know that you can tee up anywhere between the ball markers and a distance of two club lengths *behind* the tee markers. However, you may only take advantage of this rule when your fellow hackers have driven so many earth clods down the fairway that the area between the ball markers looks like it has been plowed for a crop of corn.

But the strategy gurus advise you to tee up at the exact spot in these two club lengths of depth that will allow you to land the ball precisely where you want. For example, you may estimate that the pin on a par-three hole is 150 yards from the ball markers and that you generally hit your five-iron 151 yards. The gurus recommend that you tee up one yard behind the ball markers so that you have a better chance of landing in the cup.

The first time you try this, you may pause and ask whether it really makes sense. First of all, the shot will be affected by wind speed, temperature, humidity, lunar phase and countless other variables beyond your control. On top of that, your swing itself is largely beyond your control. On one swing, your five iron could imitate a sand wedge and send the ball 151 yards straight up. On the very next swing, the same club could connect with the center of the ball, sending a line drive over the green and the adjacent highway as well. Despite these reservations, tee the ball one yard behind the tee markers. The members of your foursome will look at this move with curiosity. If asked, tell them that you are playing strategically. That will have them trading knowing glances with one another. Then proceed to swing just a tad harder than normal to offset the additional yard of distance that you have created for yourself. This will create just enough breeze from your whiff to topple the ball from your tee. Because of your strategic tee placement, you have just accomplished a drive of minus one yard, a record, even for you. When you experience the laughter from your fellow golfers, you will begin to appreciate how effective this strategy will be for stopping golf.

Strategy gurus observe that you can hit your fairway shots so far that you leave yourself with approach shots that are too short. That's right "too short". The theory here is that a short chip has to be hit with a soft, half swing that can't achieve the backspin needed to make the ball stick or at least stay on the green. The gurus recommend that you should lay up at the distance that allows you to use the club that you prefer for pitching, the club that you can always count on to land accurately and stop quickly. On hearing this advice, consider whether you really have such a club. Can you rely on *any* club in your bag to produce the same shot twice in a row?

But pretend that you actually have a club that is consistent and dependable. Deliberately place your ball short, say 100 yards from the green, so that you can take a full, back-spin-producing swing with this non-existent club. You will have your doubts about this tactic since you know that a lot can go wrong in 100 yards. But that is exactly why the strategic approach shot is so effective for creating the disgust needed to permanently stop golfing. In fact, you know that you could easily take three or four hits from 100 yards out and still not hit the green therefore forcing you to take a half swing on your approach shot anyway.

Strategy for Quitting

To stop golfing, you must pretend that you have some control of your shots. Intentionally try to lay up short in keeping with your plans to execute classic, green-biting approach shots. Watch in horror as your "safe shots" land in water hazards and sand traps. The gaping chasm between your vision and reality will help you ultimately implement your strategy to stop golfing.

10

Play Mystic

"They say that golf is like life, but don't believe them. It's more complicated than that."

—*Gardner Dickinson*

Golf is only partly about swing mechanics, scientific cure-alls and left-brain fixes. Once you are satisfied that you will never master the physical aspects of the game, try the metaphysical.

Golf as a Spiritual Quest

Some golfers are anxious to believe that golf is more than just a game. Perhaps that's because games are supposed to be fun while golf provides endless torment. It has not occurred to these people that golf might simply be a bad game.

In *Golf and the Spirit*, M. Scott Peck gives these golfers hope by arguing that golf is like life because it presents us with obstacles and challenges. In addition, golf is a good way to practice skills needed for everyday life, like self-control, humiliation and colorful language.

The theory that golf is more than just a game is one that the manufacturers of golf clubs and the builders of golf courses would like to see popularized. That's because the golf industry knows that most golfers hate golf. It also knows that the game is so excruciatingly slow that golfers have lots of time to ask questions…questions that are dangerous to the survival of the game. Why am I spending all my time and money on this game? Why do I keep torturing myself? Why am I dressed this way?

Peck supports the notion that golf is more than just a game by demonstrating the effect that golf can have on your spirit. Of course, you are well aware that golf can be very devastating to your spirit. Peck readily admits that playing golf is humiliating. In fact, he declares that golf is mortifying, or something so humiliating that death seems like an appealing alternative. He compares golf with the Roman Catholic practice of mortification in which the very faithful subject themselves to painful acts in order to combat their egos. Peck does not go so far as to claim that any monasteries require vows of golf, forcing monks to play round after round until a million of their egos could dance on the head of a pin. However, as a form of masochism, golf apparently ranks right up there with hair shirts, self-flagellation and celibacy.

Peck makes this comparison not to discourage you from playing golf but to argue that golf makes you a better person. Golf helps you empty your self of self. And this is apparently good. Peck discloses that he would probably not suffer the humiliation and mortification of the game if he didn't look at golf as a form of spiritual discipline. By the way, Peck is quite serious about this. He is not slyly suggesting that you use golf as an excuse to disappear every Sunday to attend "18 holes of worship".

Peck really looks at golf as a means to spiritual growth. With that thought in mind, ask yourself these questions as you try to stop golfing. Isn't the humiliation that you get at work and at home really sufficient for you to feel pretty fit spiritually? Isn't 18 holes a week more mortification than you really need to beat your ego to a pulp? Isn't the self-mutilation known as golf appropriate only for those trying to achieve sainthood?

The Art of Paradox

While golf can pump up your spiritual muscles, your spiritual strength can likewise improve your golf game. However you must first practice the art of paradox. Paradox is better known in the Western Hemisphere as nonsense. But that's because Westerners only know one koan: "What is the sound of one hand clapping." On hearing that, most Westerners think back to the meager applause at their piano recital or their speech to the board of directors and brood for awhile. They don't ponder the deeper meaning. Westerners feel smug about the fact that they know how to clap, so the question is irrelevant.

This is unfortunate because Peck's book is full of riddles that promise to improve your game if you could just understand them. For example, Peck urges you to "act out of the emptiness of not knowing" and to "strive and don't strive." However, he recognizes that these are not user-friendly swing thoughts. So he discusses a form of meditation in which you are not asleep but not thinking either. Peck cautions that it is difficult to stay awake and still not be thinking despite the fact that millions of people do it every day at work.

At the instant that club meets ball, Peck advocates ridding yourself of concerns, self-loathing, shame, remorse and the suspicion that your opponent "forgot" a stroke on the last hole. At that moment of impact, your mind should be like a still pond of water, free of any ripples. Apparently, when you empty yourself of your self, you make room for something else to step in and complete your shot. But unfortunately, because you have become mindless at this point, you really don't know who or what this substitute might be. Peck assumes that God takes over. But what if the atheists are right? What if the process of evolution completes your shot? If that happens, you could wait several million years for the random mutation needed to cure your slice.

Be the Ball (as Well as Everything Else in the Universe)

You have probably heard the zen-golf mantra "Be the ball", as immortalized by the movie *Caddy Shack*. In *The Cosmic Laws of Golf (and everything else),* author Printer Bowler, a believer in the oneness of the universe, reminds you that you already *are* the ball. You just may not have noticed the resemblance yet.

As well as being the ball, you are also the cup, the green, the course and everything else in the cosmos. Experiencing this oneness can be useful not just to achieving enlightenment but, more importantly, to sinking incredibly long putts.

To do this, Bowler suggests that you practice various exercises. In one, you imagine each putt as a date between the ball and the cup. Bowler claims that these two misfits desperately want to connect and become one. They have a natural, passionate attraction, he asserts. Just by looking at them, you can tell they were made for each other. The details of this torrid coupling are too explicit for a family book. Let's just say that after considerable foreplay, this exercise climaxes with the ball in the cup, leaving everyone involved, including you the golfer, very satisfied.

But, on closer examination, Bowler's exercise seems like a Hollywood scriptwriter's version of the dating scene. In Bowler's opinion, all cups are easy. In reality, the cup might be waiting for the "right ball." Possibly the cup has had a bad experience with other balls. Maybe the cup is turned off by the ball's pasty, pockmarked complexion. Or perhaps the ball doesn't particularly want to perform in the blazing sunlight of a hot afternoon. In other words, when you use this technique, your putting results could be sadly reminiscent of your own dating experiences.

Multiple Selves

In *The Inner Game of Golf*, W. Timothy Gallwey argues that we have at least two selves trying to golf at the same time. Self 1 is that obnoxious self that is constantly talking inside your head, giving you advice and berating you. Self 2, according to Gallwey, is your mute, long-suffering body, which could learn how to golf without any help from Self 1 if Self 1 would just shut up. To keep Self 1 quiet, you need to distract it with little tasks. For example, have Self 1 say "back" when you are at the top of your back swing, "hit" when the club makes impact and "stop" when you complete your follow through. You may not think that this is very absorbing. But apparently Self 1 is easily distracted.

Gallwey urges us to stop controlling, abusing and doubting ourselves and enter a state that he calls relaxed concentration. He explains that relaxed concentration occurs when Self 2 is free of Self 1. To achieve this state, Gallwey suggests a game called "fun-o" in which you just hit the ball whatever way is the most fun. In theory, by enjoying the game, Self 2 will inevitably learn how to play. However, you may find that your Self 2 enjoys "fun-o" just a little too much. Your Self 2 might be perfectly content to hit the ball with wild roundhouse swings and watch as the random hooks and slices terrorize golfers on adjacent holes. After a few years of this, you may have to admit that Self 1 was right: Self 2 is nothing but a hacker.

True Enlightenment

To quit forever, you must prove to your subconscious that you not only tried to become a spiritual person but you also tried to use your newfound spirituality for the higher calling of golf. You must demonstrate that it doesn't help to empty your self of self because whoever or whatever steps into that space may not golf any better than you. And you must show that it does not help to become the ball. Your ball doesn't want you stealing its identity. In fact, your ball would rather not even be seen with you.

11

Be Confident

In keeping with the Paradox of Golf, having confidence in your ability to play golf is sure to shatter your confidence. To finally quit, convince your subconscious that confidence can only be based on true ability. Consequently, confidence only works for those who don't need it.

Your Actual Abilities

The titles of some books and training approaches give the impression that good golf is simply a matter of having confidence. This message has great appeal. It implies that you only need to think you are good and you will be good. But once you are reading these books or attending these training sessions, you find out some of the grim details.

To achieve a state of confidence, you need to remind yourself of how hard you have practiced and how well you have played in the past. As soon as you find this out, the confidence approach to golf has the exact opposite effect that you had hoped for. Even if you have practiced, you can never practice enough. So when the instructor says that you should think about all this practice and relax, you actually consider yourself to be totally unprepared and begin to feel anxious. And when you think about how you have played in the past, you break out in a cold sweat.

The confidence technique can also ruin the relationship between your mind and body. Some confidence gurus advise you to trust your body to properly execute golf shots. However, your mind has no reason to trust your body. Repeatedly, your body has sprayed shots into trees and adjacent fairways for no apparent reason. Your mind feels justified in not trusting your body.

Your body can sense this distrust and it reacts accordingly. It plays little tricks on your mind just to "pull your mind's chain". This can lead to tensions and even open hostility. Your mind may make your body go to the driving range and hit bucket after bucket of balls under a blazing sun. Your body might retaliate by developing a windmill swing that produces random hooks and slices with no pre-dictability. Soon, with the exception of four-letter words, your mind and body aren't speaking to one another. Before long, there is talk of a trial separation. This again highlights the irony of the confidence approach. It only works on golfers who don't need it. Dwell on that before every shot for maximum golf-quitting effect.

Be Positive

If you can't have confidence, at least eliminate negative thoughts from your game advise the gurus. One, for example, urges you to jot down all the negative things that you say to yourself in an average round. Things like "You couldn't drop a putt to save your life." Then, next to each of these negative statements you are to write down a more accurate statement about that aspect of your game. This exercise is meant to help you feel good about yourself. But, as with other confidence-building techniques, it can backfire. For example, after a typical round of golf, I wrote down these negative self-criticisms followed by more accurate statements. Next to "You couldn't stay in the fairway if it was a mile wide," I wrote "You *could* stay on the fairway if it was a mile wide." Next to "You couldn't hit a green if you were standing on it," I wrote "Once I am on the green, I often stay on it." And next to "You couldn't get par on a par 20 hole," I wrote "I sometimes par holes. Just last year I got a par." In other words, this exercise helped me to realize that the negative things I say to myself on the golf course, while terribly destructive, are really quite accurate. Again this proves that there is nothing like a confidence-building technique to destroy your confidence.

You can also apply these positive, but truthful, statements before your shots. For example, before your tee shot you should say something like "After this drive, I will be closer to the hole than I am now." Chances are you will be able to make this statement a reality. But sooner or later, you will realize that these positive statements only highlight the pathetic nature of your game. Use these feelings of self-loathing to help you quit the game for good.

Quitting with Confidence

You will be greatly disappointed if you have confidence that is not supported by actual ability. Similarly, you will experience extreme self-loathing if you admit your actual lack of ability. Either approach, when applied year after humiliating year, should give you all the confidence you need to quit the game forever.

12

Have a Vision

"Why am I using a new putter? Because the last one didn't float too well."

—*Craig Stadler*

Using visualization, some golfers recreate shots that they have pictured in their minds. The trick of course is to replicate only the good visions and ignore those involuntary premonitions of disaster that spring to your mind during your back swing. Prove to your subconscious that the only vision worth realizing is the one of you flinging your last golf club into the water hazard on the last hole you will ever play.

Visualization Therapy

In *From 60 Yards In,* Ray Floyd urges you to visualize your way to better golf. With the visualization approach, you picture yourself playing good golf and your body mysteriously tries to make this fantasy into reality. This method is popular with high handicappers because they erroneously assume that they no longer have to take lessons or go to the driving range to improve their game. But the visualization technique should be equally popular with those wanting to quit golf. That's because the stark contrast between dreams and reality makes visualization therapy much more effective than simply playing poorly without any mental preparation. When you don't visualize beforehand, you only feel irritated, or at best humiliated by your lack of skill. With visualization therapy, you create false hope, leaving you that much further to fall when you actually begin swinging the club. Your frustration is intensified, knowing that you actually convinced yourself that you could play well, as illustrated in the following example.

The night before your next round of golf, excuse yourself right after dinner and go to your bedroom. Take out the scorecard for the golf course that you are about to play. Then shoot a perfect round of golf in your mind. Picture yourself driving the green on the first hole, regardless of the fact that it is more than 400 yards. Imagine yourself sinking a 40-foot putt to start your day with an eagle. Continue in this way for the remaining 17 holes, sinking chip shots, dropping impossible putts and following the sharp angles of double doglegs like a cruise missile. If you fail to play this imaginary round of golf in less than 50 strokes, try again until you do. And remember to actually record your strokes on your scorecard. Then immediately turn out the lights and fall asleep. Hopefully, your brain will be confused into thinking that you have actually played a perfect round of golf. Ideally, you will dream of applauding galleries and glimpse yourself making a humble acceptance speech as you hoist a trophy over your head.

The next morning, avoid thinking about why you feel so good about yourself. Accept your vague feeling of euphoria without question. And most importantly, keep your golf date! Some would-be quitters feel so good that they fail to proceed to step two and actually show up at the golf course. This is extremely counterproductive. This technique could exacerbate your problem if you don't play the round in reality after imagining it your mind.

On the way to the golf course, play your car radio at maximum volume, preferably using a pre-recorded tape with the theme song from a tacky sports movie. On the first tee, remember the 400-yard drive that you pictured the night before with your blanket pulled up to your chin. Then, as you follow through from that first tee shot, watch carefully as your ball takes off at a right angle from the true line, frightening the golfers trying to putt on the 9th green. As those golfers glare at you, recognize that the perfect round in your head bears no resemblance to the round that you are about to play on an actual golf course. Re-visualize each of the 18 holes. Remember the perfect strokes of the previous night and contrast them with the images that now come to your mind: drives that barely clear the end of the tee, wedge shots that bury themselves in sand bunkers and putts that leave you even further from the hole. If you are like most golfers, your body will instinctively recreate your second visualization rather than the one that you had the previous night.

Bear in mind that visualization therapy works best with repeated and regular use. Do not stop using this technique each time you are disgusted with yourself. Continue treatment until the mere sight of a scorecard creates the same self-hatred that you now are only able to experience while actually playing the game.

The Well-Planned Round

In *Mind Over Golf*, Dr. Richard Koop adds an extra consideration to the concept of planning for a round of golf. According to Dr. Koop, some golfers know that they will become anxious when they find themselves in difficult situations, leading to poor shots and counter-productive self-abuse. If that sounds familiar, Dr. Koop suggests that you write a script giving yourself a positive self-talk monologue to help you through these situations. For example, let's say you always berate yourself when you land in a bunker, putting yourself in a terrible mental state just when you need to stay calm to escape the sand. Your script here might include some happy talk about how much you love the sand and how good you are at blasting out. In other words, your script is a pack of lies. But you memorize it, rehearse it and perfect your performance until even you are convinced.

If you find an entire round of golf to be a difficult situation, your script might include every conceivable shot on the course: from the tee, in the rough, in the woods, in the sand, on the green, still on the green and so forth. Each speech could correspond with the visuals that you have also created for this round using the procedure mentioned above. Consequently, before you ever set foot on the course, you will have your ideal scenario for the round with audio as well as video.

Again, it will be tempting to skip the game itself and simply recite your lines at home. But, for maximum embarrassment, play the game and compare your script to the reality of the game. Before you even leave the first tee, you will resort to ad libs. By the second hole, the script will be tossed. And by the third green, you will be making it up as you go along.

Visualize Your Golf-Free Life

Once you have reached this point, employ Part Two of the visualization treatment. To prepare yourself for Part Two, consider why you have been unable to quit golf to date. Perhaps it's partly because you have not visualized yourself free of golf. Begin to do that now. Whenever you have the urge to play a round of golf, visualize yourself doing something else that is useful or actually fun.

If you fish, for example, do you berate yourself over your bad casts? If the fish aren't biting, do you curse like a madman and throw your rod and reel overboard? Do you come back from a day of fishing wishing that you had gone to work instead?

If fishing is not an alternative for you, think of something else. Imagine yourself hiking or just taking a walk. When you walk, you don't have to think about stance, grip, back swing and a million other counterintuitive movements. Your mind is free to consider happier thoughts and maybe even think about the place where you are walking. You rarely "don't walk well" unless you forget to alternate feet. This is an activity that feels natural. It's something that you truly can do instinctively. As proof, you almost never swear at yourself for not walking up to your potential.

Once you have visualized yourself performing alternatives to golf, compare them with your visualizations of a day on the course. If you do it right, mowing the lawn will eventually become more appealing to you than a round of golf. After you mow the lawn, you have a nicely mowed lawn. You have actually accomplished something tangible. Conversely after you have golfed, you have nothing to show for those hours. You may even shred your scorecards after every round to prevent anyone from stumbling across them while rummaging in your bag looking for tees.

Let's say that your alternative vision is nothing more exciting than dozing on your couch in front of the TV set. It's true that you accomplish nothing on the couch. In fact you probably inflict some damage on your body if you consume a six pack and one or two bags of chips. But compare that physical damage to the psychological damage inflicted by a round of golf. When you are cured of your addiction, you will clearly see that an afternoon on the couch is not only more enjoyable but ultimately better for you than a day of torment on the links.

The Ultimate Vision

Envisioning yourself playing golf well will help you stop playing golf for good. Over the course of several years, the vast discrepancy between your head game and your real game will help you achieve your ultimate vision of a golf-free life.

13

Join a Golf Community

Some golfers blame their poor scores on the courses they play rather than themselves. Play the best courses. Join a country club. Better yet move into a golf community and devote every waking moment to the game. Prove to your subconscious once and for all that the quality of the course you play has no effect on the quality of your play.

Play Better Golf Courses

Perhaps you have claimed that playing public golf courses has been hard on your handicap. Ask yourself if that's really true. No doubt the concrete tees have created a psychological disadvantage. For example, it's hard to place your ball on that plastic tube and shuffle your spikes on the rubber mats while pretending that you are actually Tiger Woods teeing up at Augusta National for the start of the Masters. On the other hand, you can get a very generous bounce off those rubber mats whenever your driver catches only the top millimeter of your ball.

Similarly, the dry fairways on many public courses don't give you the easy lies that you see on televised tournaments. But, on the other hand, you've probably produced some of the longest shots of your life on these rock-hard fairways: 50 yards in the air, 100 yards of bounce and another 100 yards of roll.

And you've had to putt on public-course turf that's so pocked and trampled you are tempted to continue using your wedge after you are already on the green. But, admit it, it helps when the municipality can afford only one tree per hole.

And it's also nice to find out that the water hazard shown on the scorecard is really just a damp depression that offers a better lie than the fairway.

But let's pretend that you actually believe that you would play better golf if you played better golf courses. You must prove to yourself that this belief is wrong if you want to stop playing for good. For example, call Pebble Beach Golf Course on the Monterey Peninsula of California. The green fees alone are astronomical. However, the only way mere mortals can play here is to stay at the Pebble Beach Lodge, which could double the cost of a round. Assuming that you don't live nearby, it may cost you anywhere from $100 to $1,000 in travel expenses to get to the golf course. So, you could easily spend $1,000 for this round of golf or $55 per hole.

In addition to monetary distress, the Pebble Beach Golf Course will inflict the necessary psychic pain. Multi-million-dollar mansions flank many fairways of this course. These aren't like the stucco condos that you are used to hitting with your banana slice. In a worst case scenario, one errant shot could shatter a crystal lawn dwarf and ricochet through a stained glass window, taking out a 16th Century vase inside.

Then you come to the hard holes. There is the famous 17th, a good example of course architect humor. It's only a par 3, a mere 178 yards. But you tee off into the wind toward a green seemingly surrounded by the crashing Pacific Ocean. The waters are so rich with golf balls here that it should be called the Great Balata Reef.

The 18th hole at Pebble Beach is basically designed to give your pride one last kick before sending you to the showers. It hugs the Pacific Ocean for its entire 543-yard length, giving good golfers at least three chances to send a shot out to sea. If you hook, make sure that the rest of this course has not depleted your ball supply by the time you arrive here. The only consolation is that the green is so close to the clubhouse that you can actually walk to the bar and chug a martini in the time needed to tally your strokes for the hole.

For best results, you should play humiliating courses, like Pebble Beach, regularly. When you only play a course once, the professional staff never gets to know you. But when you keep coming back, you will eventually be recognized, greatly increasing the potential for embarrassment. For example, by your third or fourth visit to Pebble Beach, the starter will introduce you to everyone in the pro shop as the guy who lost an entire box of golf balls on a single hole.

Join a Country Club

A country club membership will cost even more than monthly trips to Pebble Beach. And, as an added benefit, the disgrace never ends.

To create an entirely hypothetical example, let's say you join a country club. One day you card a 25 on the third hole of this country club. This is extremely embarrassing. But, because you are a member, now you have to tough it out. Your story is told over and over until it becomes local lore: "The Legend of the Third Hole Hacker". Occasionally, someone in your own foursome will tell the story, not knowing that you are the protagonist. The first few times this happens, you reveal yourself to your fellow golfers. They look at you skeptically. Some think you are just trying to impress them by claiming to be this mythic figure. Others unfortunately assume that you are lying since your golfing is even worse than that described in the Legend. Eventually the Legend sounds more like a fairy tale, with you taking 100 or more strokes. At this point, you don't even try to correct the record or reveal yourself as this monumental duffer. You simply smile and wonder how much it will cost you to cancel your membership.

Perpetual Humiliation

As a member of a country club, it is possible to be something other than a golfer. You can go home to a place where your neighbors don't know that you are the Third Hole Hacker and may not even know that you try to golf.

But when you live in a golf community, your entire life is golf. You live on a fairway. You eat many of your meals in the clubhouse restaurant. Your social contacts are primarily with other golf community denizens. Your golfing embarrassments are posted on web sites and even scrolled across the community's public access cable channel.

Consequently, in a golf community, you are likely to encounter the Legend of the Third Hole Hacker not just on the 3rd hole, but everywhere. Your kids might come home from school and ask you if there really is a Third Hole Hacker. You could overhear the story being recounted at the next table in the clubhouse restaurant. In fact the restaurant might even name a sandwich after you.

But golf communities have much more to offer than just the opportunity for non-stop humiliation, 24 hours a day. These communities are also a great way to maximize golf-related debt. They commonly feature five-bedroom, ten-bathroom mini castles priced in the "low seven figures". And those are the starter homes.

Many golf communities give new meaning to the term "conspicuous consumption." After all, they are catering to people who can afford to spend most of their waking hours hitting a ball into and out of trees. Surely these people can afford separate garages for golf carts, custom-built swimming pools in the shape of pitching wedges and full-size, indoor driving ranges.

These communities typically have gates and guard stations with security personnel on duty 24 hours a day, presumably preventing the smuggling of cheap wine into the complex. Their gymnasiums often feature work out equipment designed exclusively for golfers, such as a weight machine that isolates the muscle groups used when heaving a set of clubs into a water hazard. And the on-premise health spas often provide unique golf-related treatments, like massages that focus on the jaw and other body parts most likely to be overworked during a round of golf.

The Cost of Quitting

You may be overwhelmed by the cost of buying into a golf community, paying the monthly dues and consuming conspicuously enough to convince others that you can afford to be there. This could force you to work harder and put in longer hours at the office. Your harder work schedule may make it more difficult for you to actually golf, creating a whole new source of agitation in your life. To have any time left at all for golf, you may have to spend less time with your spouse and family. That creates a second tension dynamic which threatens your marriage and ultimately your entire outlook on life. In other words, golf could leave you broke, weary and alone as well as humiliated. This should be sufficient motivation for you to finally move into a community that prohibits golf.

14

Go Mental

"Talking to your golf ball won't do you any good. Unless you do
it while your opponent is teeing off."

—*Bruce Lansky*

Some golfers are able to hypnotize themselves so that their brains don't interfere
with the extremely complex golf swing. Self-hypnosis won't improve your game.
But it might help you believe your game has improved. Better yet, though self-
hypnosis, you might convince yourself that you are golfing when, in fact, you are
doing something that's actually fun.

The Golfer's Brain

Near the start of *Golf: The Mind Game*, author Marlin M. Mackenzie explains
that a golfer's brain sends and receives hundreds of messages during the course of
a single swing. I suspect that he is referring to the brain of a good golfer. For a
hacker, the brain probably handles thousands of messages in a single swing, most
of them wrong numbers.

For example, the brain of a normal golfer might get one message from his
body that his back swing is too fast. In response, the normal golfer might send
one message back to his body to deal with it, something simple like "Slow down."
But in the brain of a hacker, this simple exchange becomes a debate. When the
body reports that the back swing is too fast, the hacker's brain just can't let it go.
"Of course the back swing is too fast. It's *always* too fast. It's no wonder you can
never hit the ball. You look like you're chopping wood." The body has heard all
this before. It doesn't really expect to get any meaningful commands from the
brain. But just to taunt the brain, it sends a second message. Something like,

"Transmission could not be understood. Please repeat instructions." The brain gets steamed, knowing very well that the body is up to its usual tricks. "Slow down the back swing" the brain finally replies. But this has taken so much time that the body can gleefully respond "Too late. Downswing already commenced. Would you like to abort swing?" This drives the brain crazy. "Abort the swing? When have I ever aborted a swing?" "You've aborted lots of swings." "I have not." "You aborted a swing just last month, remember?" Flustered, the brain stammers: "Just hit the ball and let me do the thinking." But of course, by this time the body has already hooked the drive into the woods.

The bad news is that the messages simulated in the paragraph above deal only with swing speed. Equally intense arguments ensue regarding club angle, hand position, hip rotation, eye contact, wrist snap and hundreds of other fragments of the shot. If the brain had to consciously deal with all these messages, golfers would go crazy. And as we all know, golfers *do* go crazy trying to process all these messages.

Mindless Golf

According to Mackenzie, the golf swing should ideally occur unconsciously, or mindlessly. Chances are, you often think of yourself as golfing *mindlessly*, probably with disastrous results. Now go to Mackenzie's book and learn the right procedures for mindless golf.

In mindless golf, you establish cues that can be triggered to recreate your best shots. You may find that discouraging at first if, like me, you have never executed a shot worthy of repeating.

But Mackenzie has a solution to this problem called the "Get It" process. Let's say you have had no personal success with a particular shot, or with golf as a whole. You can still succeed by vicariously experiencing someone else's shot. By this, Mackenzie does not mean that you should throw your clubs out and simply watch the Golf Channel. He means that you should watch another golfer making a great shot using an imaginary movie on an imaginary screen. Then you should put yourself in that movie and feel yourself executing that shot over and over until you "get it". And most importantly, while watching this imaginary movie of some other golfer who then turns into you, playing scratch golf no less, try not to have a psychotic episode.

Mackenzie suggests that you could use anyone to star in your imaginary movie. But, why gamble with unknown newcomers, like your golfing partners, unless you're producing a comedy. Take your cue from the client in Mackenzie's book. Sign Tiger Woods to play the role of the First Golfer. And your part, Second Golfer, will probably be your first big movie role. So make sure the script gives you some character development and believable dialog.

Self Hypnosis

Once you feel comfortable with imaginary movies, you can proceed to self-hypnosis. The process of self-hypnosis puts you in a trance. This is not the kind of trance that you might find yourself in after you miss a one-foot putt and stare into space long enough to frighten your fellow golfers. Mackenzie refers to that kind of rage-induced, catatonic state as a "negative trance".

As you might guess, negative trances create negative results. On the other hand, positive trances produce positive results. You don't have to wave your putter back and forth like a pendulum to put yourself in a trance. According to Mackenzie, you can put yourself in a trance by using a swing thought as a mantra. Alternatively, you can go mindless just by staring at your golf ball. But remember only to stare, not glare. After you drive two tee shots out of bounds, you may be tempted to glare at the next ball you tee up. Avoid that temptation since the trance produced by a glare will probably be negative.

The best subjects for hypnosis are able to relax and empty their minds of all concerns and other thoughts. Perhaps you meet this criterion. At work you sometimes don't have a single thought in an entire day, and you aren't even trying to empty your mind.

However, good subjects must also believe. They must believe not just in hypnosis itself but in their ability to comply with the suggestions made while under hypnosis. A case in point would be the stage hypnotists who you may have run across at office parties. These entertainers don't ask their subjects to speak foreign languages or solve complicated math problems in their heads. This is partly because it's no fun to see the hypnotized subjects look smart when all their coworkers want them to make fools of themselves. But mostly it's because the hypnotist has got to stick to things that these people can actually do, like imitate a chicken or take their clothes off.

Chances are, you have never seen a stage hypnotist ask someone in a trance to swing a golf club. The golf swing is too complex. When asked to produce a golf swing most hypnotized subjects would pretend not to understand the command and simply imitate a chicken or take their clothes off. The stage hypnotist knows better than to ask someone to do something they can't do. That's why you can empty your mind till it has fewer thoughts than your stomach. But it won't help.

You wouldn't believe in your ability to produce a good golf swing even if you had your mind surgically removed.

Case Study: Tiger Woods

In *Think Like Tiger*, John Andrisani discusses two possible explanations for Tiger Woods' extraordinary ability to concentrate under the most stressful circumstances. First, Tiger was introduced to Zen meditation techniques as a child with the help of his mother, who was born in Thailand. He reportedly learned how to enter a state of complete relaxation in a Buddhist temple. According to Andrisani, this allows him to achieve "harmony among the mind, body and sprit." Andrisani points out that Buddhist's do not expect any rewards from enlightenment, other than enlightenment. But, as a nice bonus, meditation has helped Tiger Woods become the only golfer to hold all four major tournament championships at the same time. Andrisani writes that Tiger's serenity on the course "reflects the oneness of the universe that comes from meditation." Perhaps. But maybe that serenity also reflects the fact that Tiger's earnings already exceed $41 million.

Andrisani's book goes on to say that Tiger's concentration may be attributable to hypnosis as well as meditation. Starting at age ten, Tiger's coaching team included Dr. Jay Brunza, a clinical psychologist who confirmed to Andrisani that he had hypnotized Tiger Woods. Interestingly, Dr. Brunza caddied for Tiger in 36 tournaments from 1991 to 1996. Tiger won 33 of these 36 matches. This may cause you to take greater care before you select your next caddie. Don't just make sure he has a caddie badge and a clean tee shirt. Ask about his post-graduate degrees and whether he specializes in sports psychology.

Today, Tiger is a multi-millionaire and would probably rather have a stock-broker rather than a sports psychologist by his side at all times. Some critics are under the impression that self-hypnosis is an unfair shortcut to Tiger-like golfing. But, in addition to mind control, Woods started golfing at the age of two and from then on devoted practically his entire life to lessons, practice ranges and endless rounds of golf. If that's a shortcut, what's the hard way?

The painful truth is that hackers under hypnosis don't become Tiger Woods. They become hackers in a trance. Luckily, most golfers seem to know this intuitively. The game could change radically if golfers started visiting their neighborhood hypnotherapists before every round. If all 30 million golfers in this country started slicing and hooking in a trance, courses could become even more dangerous than they are now. Manufacturers might respond with helmets and padding to protect the most vulnerable parts of the body. The sport might attract a whole new breed of extreme golfers. Thrill seekers, bored with sky diving, would dare each other to golf. These new daredevils could more than offset the cowardly golfers who flee the game after one or two skull fractures. In other words, the unfortunate result of widespread hypnosis could be a spike in the golf pandemic.

The Club-Free Swing

Mackenzie observes that the best golf swings are free and effortless. You can trigger feelings of freedom and effortlessness in your body by creating what Mackenzie calls a "free-swing anchor". First, recall a time in your life when you experienced complete freedom. Then play a scene from that carefree time onto your golf gloves as you grip the club. As that image relaxes your body, swing the club using your newly found freedom. Mackenzie claims that golfers pick different times in their life for their image of freedom: pre-marriage, pre-kids or pre-workaday adulthood. But, for those who have been bedeviled by golf, the time of life that most vividly represents freedom has got to be pre-golf.

When you are ready to finally quit golf, project a scene from your pre-golf life on your golf gloves. Savor the relaxation radiating from your hands to your arms. When you feel the complete freedom of your pre-golf life throughout your entire body, take a slow, easy swing and let the club slide out of your hands and sail into a landfill. Repeat that process until you are rid of all your clubs and finally free of golf.

When You Wake Up

When you are finally at the end of your ten-year course of treatment, hypnosis can be very instrumental in helping you quit the game forever. While in a trance, tell yourself that you feel violently ill when you even think of golf. Say that the mere sight of a golf course makes you start cursing and writhing in agony. Tell yourself that the golf club is painful to hold and an instrument of misery. You will have no trouble believing any of these suggestions because they are all true. Then, tell yourself that the instant you hear a snapping sound, you will awaken from your trance feeling refreshed and forever free of the desire to golf. Then awaken and find that the snap that brought you out of your trance was the sound of your last golf club breaking over your knee.

15

Complete the Course of Treatment

"Golf is played by twenty million mature American men whose wives think they are out having fun."

—*Jim Bishop*

Quitting golf is hard work. You must systematically and repeatedly try every conceivable way to improve your game in order to convince yourself, once and for all, that your game will never improve.

- Take Lessons—Pay an instructor to tell you that your body already knows how to golf instinctively even though your body has demonstrated repeatedly that it has no aptitude for golf and, therefore, never will.

- Get Scientific—Analyze why golf is considered a sport instead of a game of chance when scientific studies prove that less than one of three perfect putts drops and only one golf ball in 24 can even travel in a straight line.

- Buy New Equipment—Give your subconscious no opportunity to insinuate that you could have broken 100 if you had just spent more on plutonium-tipped drivers, diamond-faced wedges and other miracles-du-jour.

- Read Golf Books—Learn that reading just a fraction of the 40,000 golf books currently available will not help your game one bit although it *would* have the beneficial effect of keeping you off the course for several years.

- Alter Your Personality—Control your fear, anger, depression, self-consciousness and laziness. Then ponder why you would put that monumental achievement at risk by trying to golf.

- Subscribe to Golf Magazines—Notice that each issue features new tips for curing the same problems that were supposedly cured by the tips in the previous issues.

- Get Strategic—Find out how to heighten the disappointment of each lousy shot by pretending that you can have some control over where your ball will go.

- Play Mystic—Relinquish control of the club and discover that whoever or whatever completes your swing can't golf any better than you.

- Be Confident—Discover that having confidence in your ability to golf is the surest way to shatter your confidence.

- Have A Vision—Experience the enhanced humiliation caused by an actual round of golf after you have pictured a perfect round of golf in your mind.

- Join A Golf Community—Spend lavishly on a golf-centric home and lifestyle that forces you to work two or three jobs, leaving you absolutely no time to actually play golf.

- Go Mental—Employ self-hypnosis to convince yourself that you are a better golfer or, better yet, to convince yourself that you are playing golf when in fact you are doing something that's actually fun.

Applying these remedies once will provide only temporary relief. To stop golfing permanently, you must complete the full course of treatment. That means taking regular doses of the prescription summarized in this book for the *full ten years.*

Why not quit immediately? As explained throughout this book, the power of self-delusion is too strong. You consciously know that the game is pointless and that you will never be good at it. But some deviant part of your subconscious continues to believe that you could play a round of golf without embarrassment "if only." If only you had taken more lessons. If only you had bought new equipment, and so on. Remember that your subconscious is not capable of language or abstract thought. Logic will not affect it. Your subconscious will persist in giving you false hope unless you bludgeon it year after year with the raw emotion of disappointment, frustration and humiliation.

During this ten-year period, you may hit a good shot or two. You may even have a good hole from time to time. These are not setbacks in your recovery. They are, in fact, part of the cure. Let yourself believe that you have found the tip that pulls your whole game together. This will greatly increase your frustration when the tip no longer works and you realize that golf has jerked your chain again. It's all part of the long hard process of quitting golf.

Whatever you do, don't give up. You can quit!

Endnotes

1. Jack Nicklaus (with Ken Bowden), *Golf My Way* (New York: Fireside-Simon & Schuster, 1974), p.18.

2. Ben Hogan, *Power Golf* (New York: Pocket Books—Simon & Schuster, 1948), p. xi.

3. Harvey Penick and Bud Shrake, *Harvey Penick's Little Red Book: Lessons and Teachings from a Lifetime in Golf* (New York: Fireside—Simon & Schuster, 1992), p. 33.

4. Alan Shapiro, Ph.D., *Golf's Mental Hazards: Overcome Them and Put an End to the Self-Destructive Round* (New York: Fireside—Simon & Schuster, 1996), pp. 32-33.

5. Ibid., p. 60.

0-595-32101-1

Made in the USA
Middletown, DE
06 February 2020